What is
Philosophy?

Other *What is . . .?* books available

Linguistics
Psychology
Communication Studies
Accounting

in preparation

Engineering
Politics
Business Studies

What is Philosophy?

Trevor Pateman

Reader in Education,
University of Sussex

Edward Arnold

© Trevor Pateman 1987

First published in Great Britain 1987 by
Edward Arnold (Publishers) Ltd, 41 Bedford Square, London
WC1B 3DQ

Edward Arnold (Australia) Pty Ltd, 80 Waverley Road, Caulfield
East, Victoria 3145, Australia

Edward Arnold, 3 East Read Street, Baltimore, Maryland 21202,
USA

British Library Cataloguing in Publication Data

Pateman, Trevor
    What is philosophy?. —— (What is . . . . .?)
    1. Philosophy
    I. Title   II. Series
    100   B72

    ISBN 0-7131-6509-X

Text set in 10/11pt Times Compugraphic
by Colset Private Limited, Singapore
Made and printed in Great Britain by Richard Clay Ltd,
Bungay, Suffolk.

Contents

Preface

I have written this little book primarily with the prospective undergraduate student of Philosophy in mind. In it I have tried to avoid the tone of the recruiting sergeant or the advertising copywriter, though in Chapter 2 I have illustrated the concerns of the various sub-branches of Philosophy with examples of argument which I personally find interesting, even intriguing. So I hope something of the potential fascination of Philosophy comes through, even though I have no missionary zeal for converting every potential student of Philosophy into an actual student. Some of the drawbacks of Philosophy as a subject of study are indicated in Chapters 1 and 3.

A number of friends and colleagues were kind enough to comment on the draft of this book, or individual sections of it. I should like to thank Peter Abbs, Tony Becher, Rickie Dammann, Terry Diffey, Barbara Goodwin, Selwyn Hughes, Michael Morris and an anonymous reader at Edward Arnold for their reactions and for advice which I have not always heeded. I am also grateful to Jean Stroud for persuading me not to turn down the invitation to contribute to the *What Is . . . ?* series, and to Margaret Ralph for doing the word-processing.

Trevor Pateman

1

What Philosophy is not

1.1 Introduction

Though Philosophy can now be studied as a subject at 'A' level, following the syllabus of the Joint Matriculation Board or Associated Examining Board, very few students have the opportunity of taking this 'A' level. Consequently, most students considering Philosophy as a subject for degree study will not have encountered it previously as a taught subject. Since the grass often seems greener on the other side, it is as well to begin a book on what Philosophy is with some remarks on what Philosophy is not. For a great deal of what gets called 'Philosophy' in Universities and polytechnics has only indirect connections with what the word 'philosophy' means or suggests in everyday discussions. For convenience when I am talking about Philosophy as a subject, I shall give the word an initial capital P; when I am talking about philosophy in its everyday sense, I shall give the word a small p. And I shall call people whose job it is to teach Philosophy 'Philosophers', but designate the great philosophers of the past with a small p. I have not attempted to make any parallel distinctions when referring to other subjects.

1.2 Philosophy isn't about answers, but about questions

Arguing or discussing with a friend, we might often enough have occasion to say things like, 'It all depends what your philosophy is'. By this we mean that whether or not you evaluate some situation or event as desirable or undesirable depends on what your values are or, more generally, on what

1

your outlook on life is. Sometimes disagreements seem to arise from different political values; sometimes from what may seem to be temperamental differences in outlook: some people are optimists and others are pessimists. These different kinds or level of value and attitude also make it possible for people to take the same side on a question but for quite different reasons: I may support CND because I don't see communism as a threat; you may support it because you think it morally wrong to possess the means of mass destruction; others may support CND because they are pessimistic about our ability to control the technology we have created.

Philosophers, as ordinary citizens, are as capable of joining in such arguments as the rest of us, and of taking up positions on one side or another. But, at least until recently, most Philosophers who teach on degree courses have not thought that it is their business, as Philosophers, to take sides in political or moral debates or to espouse particular outlooks on life. They have not seen it as their job to aim at what are often called 'first-order' or 'substantive' moral or political judgements, judgements about what actually is right or wrong. Many Philosophers still take this view of the nature and limits of their subject. It is a view which has undoubtedly disappointed students who have taken up the study of Philosophy because they thought it would provide them with Answers to the large Questions about living which preoccupy them. When it was not simply irrelevant to such large Questions, Philosophy turned out to be a subject in which your Questions were met not with Answers but simply with more and more Questions. This is nicely illustrated by one of the controversies provoked by the marking policy adopted for its 'A' level in Philosophy by the Associated Examining Board, which led a number of University-based Philosophers to assert, in a letter to the press, that 'We would expect a good candidate to begin an answer with a reformulation of the question' – a view which will come as a surprise to all those 'A' level candidates who have been drilled to *Answer the Question*, not to question it!

If it does or did not aim at first-order or substantive judgements, what does Philosophy aim at? One way of characterizing the practices of Philosophers is to say that though they are or were not professionally interested in establishing what is politically or morally right, their interest is in considering the general nature of political and moral argument and of the words and concepts used in such argument. The Philosophers' questions are 'second-order' and include such questions as: Does moral and political argument differ from scientific argument and, if so, how? Can there be a right answer to questions which give rise to disagreements based in differences of moral and political value? What jobs do words like 'right' and 'good', 'wrong' and 'bad' perform in argument? Students who wanted to discuss, say, the morality of nuclear weapons would find themselves, on this approach to Philosophy, pushed back into consideration of such prior questions as, What is morality? Likewise, in an area like the Philosophy of Religion even the apparently central, defining, question – Does God exist? – can be rolled back into an examination of the language in which religious belief is expressed and the structures of theological argument. I think many students have found the encounter with such practices frustrating and have come to see it as a cop-out and not as a necessary part of their own self-clarification.

However, as I have indicated by some qualifying adjectives and the use of the past tense, it would not be true to say that all Philosophers nowadays adhere to a strictly 'second-order' conception of their subject. Many of them do see it as part of the aim of Philosophy to deliver first-order or substantive judgements, even if by routes which are often roundabout and difficult. In political Philosophy, for example, there is now a general willingness to work towards first-order conclusions, inspired by the example of a number of contemporary American Philosophers, foremost among whom is the Harvard professor, John Rawls. His book *A Theory of Justice* has dominated discussions in political Philosophy since its publication in 1970. (All works mentioned in the text are listed alphabetically in Appendix A, Part 1.) What Rawls does, in six-hundred-odd pages, is attempt to construct a watertight argument leading the reader from premises he or she can freely accept to acceptance of two fundamental principles of distributive justice. These principles specify that all persons should have the most extensive equal liberties, compatible with the same liberties for everyone, and that material inequalities among persons are only justified if they work out to the advantage of the least advantaged (the least well-off) members

4 What is Philosophy?

of society. These principles, though very general and requiring interpretation before they become applicable, are undoubtedly 'first-order' principles in a recognizable liberal democratic tradition, and they have been attacked as such by conservatives and Marxists. But the idea of trying to reach such substantive conclusions by means of a general, philosophical argument has had a profound impact on the recent practice of political Philosophy. The new willingness of Philosophers to engage in substantive arguments is evidenced in the pages of such journals as *Philosophy and Public Affairs* (USA) and the *Journal of Applied Philosophy* (UK). These journals contain detailed discussions of such issues as abortion, pornography, nuclear weapons, racial discrimination, civil disobedience and war – discussions which would have been thought outside the scope of Philosophy until quite recently, but which from the point of view of students have undoubtedly refreshed a subject which had, in parts and for a period, become quite sterile.

1.3 Philosophy isn't all about politics and morals

I must hasten to add to what I have said in the previous section that the study of Philosophy in higher education isn't primarily a study of morals, politics (or religion), whether in first-order or second-order terms. The central, and most prestigious, areas of Philosophy are those which deal with the nature of reality and our knowledge of it. For example, philosophers have always been centrally concerned with a set of questions which, once asked, always seem to tempt thinkers to sceptical answers – answers which suggest that we do not have any firm grounds for believing what has hitherto seemed obviously true: Does the world outside me really exist? If it does, can I know anything about it? Can I know anything about what is unavailable to the five senses, for example, the thoughts and feelings – the minds – of other people? No student of Philosophy can escape an encounter with some of these questions and the sceptical answers to them which have been entertained at different times. Philosophy is not a subject for anyone who cannot take the questions, or sceptical answers, with at least some degree of seriousness, some of the time, though at least one great philosopher of the past, David Hume (1711–76)* expresses an impatience with sceptical doubts:

Most fortunately it happens, that since reason is incapable of dispelling these clouds (of sceptical doubt), nature herself suffices to that purpose, and cures me of this philosophical melancholy and delirium, either by relaxing my bent of mind, or by some avocation, and lively impression of my senses, which obliterate all these chimeras. I dine, I play a game of backgammon, I converse, and am merry with my friends; and when after three or four hours' amusement, I would return to these speculations, they appear so cold, and strained, and ridiculous, that I cannot find in my heart to enter into them any farther. (Hume, *A Treatise of Human Nature*, 1739)

Hume's impatience is, however, part of his answer to scepticism. Where other philosophers, such as Descartes (1596–1650) had sought to reason their way out of sceptical doubts, Hume argues that reason is incapable of disproving sceptical positions. It is our human nature which saves us from scepticism, and makes possible the commonsense view of reality which we cannot for long resist holding. This naturalist view is one currently very congenial to Philosophers, not least because it is widely thought that one of the major philosophers of the twentieth century, Ludwig Wittgenstein (1889–1951) was, in effect, arguing for a naturalistic response to sceptical doubts and arguments. Arguments against a sceptic will always run out and to the sceptic's next 'Why?' we can only respond 'That's how we are' or 'That's how things are'. What Hume and Wittgenstein have then to persuade us is that these answers are good enough and all we need. They try to make the sceptic look like the child who goes on asking 'Why?' even after it has been given all the answers it could need or desire, so that though the next 'Why?' seems identical to the last 'Why?' there is, in fact, a break and language which was being used to some purpose up to a certain point is now being used idly.

Scepticism and naturalism are two major motifs in contemporary Philosophy which recur in discussions of knowledge, language and mind and which we shall encounter again in Chapter 2.

---

*Dates of birth and death are given on first mention of a philosopher's name. Those not given dates were alive at the time of writing.

1.4 Philosophy isn't the history of philosophy

In the previous section, I mentioned two famous philosophers of the past, Descartes and Hume, and some people are no doubt attracted to Philosophy by the prospect of reading the Great Works of the great philosophers of the past. And, fortunately for them, there is no difficulty in most Philosophy courses in spending a lot of one's time reading such Great Works. The list of great philosophers does not vary much from course to course, and you would be hard put to find a Philosophy course where you could not spend a considerable amount of time reading work by some or all of Plato (427–347 BC), Aristotle (384–322 BC), Hobbes (1588–1679), Descartes, Spinoza (1632–77), Leibniz (1646–1716), Locke (1632–1704), Berkeley (1685–1753), Hume, Kant (1724–1804), Rousseau (1712–78), Hegel (1770–1831), Nietzsche (1844–1900), John Stuart Mill (1806–73) and Marx (1818–83). The ideas of the philosophers in this list are the subject of innumerable books; short introductions to most of them can be found in Oxford University Press's *Past Masters* series. There are several things worth noting about the list.

First, it represents more or less exclusively the traditions of European philosophy. It is true that Plato and Aristotle pre-date Christianity and that Spinoza was steeped in Judaism, but it is also true that the list contains no representatives of such non-European traditions as classical Indian, Chinese, Arab or Islamic philosophy. At best, these traditions are available for study in Philosophy courses as specialized options; often enough, they are simply unavailable, because Philosophers have no interest in these traditions, except perhaps as bedtime reading. Anyone seriously interested in such non-European traditions would be well advised to follow a course in the languages, histories, cultures or geographical areas to which these philosophies belong and to forget the idea of studying Philosophy.

Second, there are no women on the list, nor would there be even if it was considerably lengthened to bring in other major figures in the history of philosophy. Though in the twentieth century, there have been distinguished women Philosophers (in America, Susanne Langer and Hannah Arendt (1906–75); in Britain, G.E.M. Anscombe and Philippa Foot, for example) it is nonetheless true that for two thousand years, up to and including its institutionalization as a subject of study in higher education, Philosophy has been pursued by and dominated by men. Many of them have been terrific sexists not just in their private lives but in their writings. This is notoriously true of Rousseau, about whom a great deal has recently been written by feminists. However, one of the philosophers on my initial list, John Stuart Mill, was an active feminist and wrote one of the classics of feminism, *The Subjection of Women* (1869). Mill even anticipated by over a hundred years the current practice of avoiding sexist language in his writing, preferring (for example) to write 'humankind' instead of 'mankind' and 'the human race' instead of 'Man'.

A student interested in sex and gender issues could spend time examining the sexism of a Rousseau or the feminism of a John Stuart Mill, but this certainly does not add up to an engagement with the totality of Philosophy's past. For feminists, a more general and central question has become the status of the central philosophical concept of reason and its relation to such concepts as that of feeling. Not only have these concepts been frequently juxtaposed by the philosophers of the past, but they have been sex-linked in various ways: reason assigned to men and feeling to women, for example. Here is certainly a large area worthy of exploration, and there are now Philosophers ready to explore it, some of them organized in 'Women in Philosophy' groups in both Britain and the USA. Nonetheless, I think that in comparison with a subject like, say, Sociology, the study of Philosophy could still be pretty unrewarding for someone whose main interests are in sex and gender issues.

Some readers may have thought that it is anachronistic to write of Rousseau as a sexist or Mill as a feminist. Isn't this simply to project a current way of thinking into a past where it does not sensibly belong? Shouldn't we read the philosophers of the past in a way which is attuned to their own time, rather than to ours? This objection brings me to the third point that I want to make in this section, namely this. Though it is true that Philosophy students spend a good deal of their time reading the Great Works of the philosophers of the past, they are not required to read them in a historian's frame of mind. Rather, the works of the past are read, primarily, for their current interest, for their bearing on the problems and positions with which contemporary Philosophers are concerned. They are read for their arguments, as is nicely illustrated by an excellent series of books published by Routledge & Kegan Paul entitled *The Arguments of the Philosophers*. For many Philosophers, the problems of Philosophy are constant or perennial, and though in the writers of the past, discussion is couched in different terms and has different emphases, still, it is argued, it is essentially the same problems which are being discussed. So, for example, Bertrand Russell wrote a little textbook of Philosophy, published in 1912 and still widely used, simply entitled *The Problems of Philosophy*.

Some Philosophers dispute that this is a satisfactory approach to the philosophy of the past, and I share some of the dissatisfaction. And, undoubtedly, it is more common nowadays for Philosophers to approach the classic texts of the past with greater historical sensitivity; to that extent, they have accepted the validity of criticisms of their a-historical approach. Nonetheless, it is important for the intending student not to confuse Philosophy with the History of Ideas or Intellectual History. The main aim of the Philosopher is not to place an idea in its context, to relate it to other currents of thought, or to trace a chain of influences; it is simply to consider whether or not ideas are coherent and true. Of course, that presupposes that you have understood the ideas in question, and the Philosopher may turn to the historian for help in understanding what is meant by some passage in a classic text – alternatively, the Philosopher becomes his or her own historian. But someone whose main interests are not in, say, Descartes' arguments, but rather in Descartes himself, his friends, his sources and his influences, should be studying History of Ideas or Intellectual History not Philosophy.

1.5 Philosophy isn't the same thing to everyone

The closer we approach to the present, the more controversial becomes the question of what Philosophy is. All Philosophers would be happy to have Plato on their syllabuses, and do, but among recent and living Philosophers there is controversy over who it is most important to read – even over who is worth reading at all. Notably, there is a polarization of view between those (including myself) who accept the dominance of what is called 'analytic Philosophy', largely shaped by the work of living American Philosophers, and those who look to the rival traditions of modern continental Philosophy. To the former group, the work of such Philosophers as W.V.O. Quine, Donald Davidson, Saul Kripke, Hilary Putnam, Daniel Dennett, John Searle, John Rawls and Robert Nozick is central. These are Philosophers whose thinking is often rooted in the achievements of modern physical science, formal logic and, more recently, computer science and artificial intelligence. In contrast, the key figures for the friends of modern continental Philosophy would include Heidegger (1889–1976), Sartre (1905–80), Merleau-Ponty (1908–61) and, among contemporaries, Jacques Derrida. All these Philosophers come out of the philosophical movement known as phenomenology and inaugurated by Husserl (1858–1938), but they are also connected to other movements of thought such as Marxism, psychoanalysis and literary theory. The atmosphere of the two traditions is quite different, and even though some authors in one camp are taken seriously by authors in the other (so, for example, Searle has been indirectly influenced by Husserl and Heidegger), the general relationship is one of mutual incomprehension or hostility (so, for example, Searle and Derrida have engaged in acid polemics in which the very claim of each to be taken seriously is at stake).

The student of Philosophy will find either that he or she is following a course which simply disregards modern continental Philosophy, or else a course where he or she will eventually have to choose on which side of the divide to work. For there are certainly very few teachers who can or want to work on both sides of the divide, and consequently there is very little opportunity for students to compare and contrast the two approaches, even where it is reasonably clear that representatives of the two approaches actually have questions and positions in common (as do Wittgenstein and Heidegger, for instance). Undoubtedly, the existence of such rival and mutually uncomprehending traditions makes it harder for students to make sense of a subject, which is in any case, never an easy one.

1.6 Philosophy isn't easy

I have said several things about Philosophy which may be read as negative comments; to say that Philosophy isn't easy must make it seem that my aim really is to put you off the subject. This is not the case. It is one of the pleasures of Philosophy that it isn't easy, though anyone who wants an easy life should really study something else (I won't suggest what . . .).

The difficulty of Philosophy arises in a number of rather different ways. First, there is the fact that no text written several hundred years ago is likely to be easy to read, and insofar as in Philosophy there are Great Works of the past to be read, they will pose problems of understanding. These should not be exaggerated: some of Plato's dialogues, Descartes' *Discourse on Method* (1637), Berkeley's *Three Dialogues Between Hylas and Philonus* (1713) are accessible enough to be gripping works.

Second, and more importantly, Philosophy is relentlessly abstract. Examples abound in philosophical argument, but they only illustrate the argument, and if you don't follow the argument, you won't see the point of the example, which will often enough simply seem silly.

Third, Philosophy has become increasingly specialized and, as in many sciences, current journal articles – which are an important part of undergraduate reading material – will assume that you already know the nature of the question to discussion of which they are making a contribution. And it is not always straightforward to find out what the question is, since Philosophy is not a subject which has a linear, sequential structure in which you can learn A, then B, then C and so on. Learning in Philosophy involves a great deal of criss-crossing over the same ground in which one tries to make more and more connections between different parts of the subject.

Fourth, the criteria of success in Philosophy are far from clear. As I have already mentioned, Philosophers have publicly disagreed over the criteria which should be used in marking 'A' level scripts and I am sure they could as readily disagree over the marking of undergraduate work. For though Philosophers, like mathematicians, often hold to an ideal of proof – to a goal of making their arguments complete and decisive – the nature of the material they are working with makes it difficult to achieve such a goal. Equally, it will rarely be clear or agreed when and whether such a goal has been achieved. In fact, despite ideals of proof and rigour, much Philosophy has a suggestive character which seeks to win intuitive assent to a series of propositions which are by no means linked in a deductive chain. But one person's compelling suggestions are another person's hand waving or whistling in the dark. Consequently, Philosophy, unlike mathematics, is unlikely to appeal to the person who likes certainty; it is much more satisfying for the person who enjoys creative uncertainty. The satisfactions of Philosophy come from finding footholds on sheer surfaces which may not, in the end, be climbable at all.

The reader who is still interested in Philosophy can now turn in the next chapter to a more systematic presentation of what Philosophy is.

2

What Philosophy is

2.1 Introduction

Students encounter Philosophy as a series of courses. These will not be the same everywhere, and both titles and content are variable. But there is enough of a common pattern to make it possible to present Philosophy through the branches which will go to making up a typical Philosophy course and this is what I offer in this chapter. My division of Philosophy into nine branches (plus two residual categories) is modelled on the divisions employed by Ted Honderich and Myles Burnyeat in their excellent Penguin anthology, *Philosophy As It Is* (1979); it also matches quite well the divisions employed by Anthony O'Hear in his valuable introduction, *What Philosophy Is* (1985). The disadvantage of my division is that it effectively pushes modern continental Philosophy into one of the residual categories. The reader should be aware that it is very much a sketch of the concerns of contemporary Anglo-American analytical Philosophy which is presented in this chapter; but those are also the main concerns of undergraduate Philosophy courses.

2.2 Metaphysics

One way of defining Metaphysics is as the study of all the question physics or, more generally, science, cannot answer. Alternatively, Metaphysics can be defined as the study of all the answers which science has to suppose are already given if science is to be possible at all.

The first definition is one which has led many, perhaps most, philosophers since Hume and Kant to regard Metaphysics as a discreditable and discredited branch of Philosophy, since in it – as the definition already indicates – one is trying to over-step the bounds of sense to answer questions which science can-not answer. But if science cannot answer them, how can they be answered at all? A traditional response was to say that reason could answer them – this was what the rationalist metaphysics of a Spinoza or Leibniz is based upon. Kant is widely thought to have discredited such metaphysics in his *Critique of Pure Reason* (1781). Another response to this ques-tion is to say that they can be answered by faith: the answer to a question such as, Does the world exist independently of our knowledge of it? is as much a matter of faith as the answer to the question, Does God exist? To answer 'No' to these ques-tions is as much to profess one's faith as to answer 'Yes'. But for Philosophers faith is very much something you fall back on when you recognize that argument and evidence cannot answer your questions, and the recourse to faith is simply proof that metaphysical questions are not amenable to regular treatment by argument and evidence.

If people would stop asking metaphysical questions, the problems of Metaphysics would not arise. Some Philosophers have indeed seen it as their task to persuade us not to *ask* metaphysical questions by, for example, getting us to see the questions as nonsensical. But whilst we can readily imagine a world in which people did not ask, Does God exist? – not because they took a positive or negative answer for granted, but because the question simply didn't arise for them – it is not so easy to imagine other questions of Metaphysics simply disappearing.

It seems that one reason why questions of Metaphysics won't go away is that the sciences themselves must always presuppose answers to certain questions they themselves do not and cannot answer. (This is how the second definition of metaphysics arises.) These questions turn out to be traditional metaphysical ones. Consider, for example, how the practice of scientific experiment presupposes an affirmative answer to questions about the uniformity of nature. When scientists repeat today the experiment they conducted yesterday, their practice only makes sense and only counts as a *repetition* of the same experi-ment against the background of an assumption that nature today will work in the self-same way as nature yesterday – that the *laws of nature* will be unchanged. In other words, it only makes sense to use experiments in an effort to find out what the laws of nature are if you assume that those laws are unchanging. But why should they be? If the laws which govern a country can change – from one day to the next, in fact – why shouldn't the laws which govern nature change, too? Why do we think it a *metaphysical impossibility* that the laws of nature should be different tomorrow from what they are today?

We are, in general, utterly convinced that when we wake up tomorrow it will be into a physical world which behaves exactly like today's world. If it doesn't because (for example) we are travellers in a space rocket, this is only because the conditions in which the laws of nature operate have changed. The laws themselves will not have changed. If you like, this is the faith of the scientist and Metaphysics is concerned with the question whether that faith can be grounded in any way – supported by reasons, evidence and argument. The opponent of Metaphysics, in the shape of a philosopher like David Hume, argues that the faith cannot be grounded and that the basis of our faith or conviction is psychological rather than rational: we cannot *help* assuming that the world in the future will be like the world in the past, but we have no *reasons* for assuming this. The uniformity of nature, for example, is not something we can demonstrate, but rather an assumption which organizes our experience and our practical activity.

Hume's specific anti-metaphysical position will become clearer if we consider for a moment his famous analysis of the relation of cause and effect in the *Treatise of Human Nature*. For Hume, relations of cause and effect are not observable parts of the world. What we can see in the world are events linked in space and succeeding each other in time. When events of one kind (A) are regularly succeeded by events of another kind (B), it is then that we are led to attribute a causal connection to them and to say that *A causes B*. But the idea of the causal link between A and B arises in us from perceptions which do not themselves show a causal relation. The idea of causality arises within us from our *imagination*, says Hume. It is not something perceived at work in the world. What we call a cause is something which gives rise to the *idea* of its being causally connected to something else. As Hume puts it in the *Treatise*:

A CAUSE is an object precedent and contiguous to another, and so united with it, that the idea of the one determines the mind to form the idea of the other.

What Hume is saying is that relations between events in the world are, as far as observation goes, like events on a VDU screen while we are playing some computer game. If we see light on the screen as moving and the collision of light points as the 'cause' of their subsequent movement or explosion, we know that this is simply the result of our way of imagining what the pattern of light on the screen represents. There are no cause and effect relations visible on the screen: we think we know that whatever causality there is in the computer program responsible for the light display. Hume's point is that we project causality into nature just as we project movement, collisions, reboundings, explosions onto the light pattern on the VDU screen. (And he would deny that there is a computer program 'behind' the real world!) It is not the world which becomes clearer to us through such reflections, but facts about our own psychology, our ways of perceiving and imagining. If you ask, for example, what the difference is between seeing light points as moving on the VDU screen and seeing light points as explosions, you will learn something about our minds, our psychology, not about computers.

As Kant saw, one major consequence of Hume's way of thinking is to make the world as it really is radically inaccessible to us. We can never know how the world *really* is because we can never get behind the appearances it presents to us in a perception, which is itself imaginatively coloured. The world of things in themselves is radically unknowable, and it is futile to speculate on the question, What is the world *really* like behind the appearances which it presents to us constituted as we are?

Suppose someone disputed this conclusion in the following way. We see objects in the world as, for example, coloured: as red, blue, and so on. We know that this is not how those objects really are, but just the way they appear to us. If we had different kinds of eyes, we would see those objects differently, as do flies and frogs. This doesn't mean to say that we cannot say what colour really is. For science provides us with a theory of light waves, reflective surfaces, and so on, which allow us to define colours objectively in terms of light-wave properties, etc. An objective definition of colour tells us what colour really is, apart from our subjective experience of its appearances.

The response to this is to point out that the problem of appearance and reality, as it has preoccupied philosophers, goes deeper than the objection allows. Colours are one class of what Philosophers call *secondary qualities* (sounds are another): they are not qualities in things themselves but in the way they appear to us, constituted as we are. And that means that they can indeed be reduced to more 'objective' or primary qualities, as the objection urges. But even when that reduction is achieved, the metaphysical problems which concern Hume and Kant simply reappear: our evidence for the way things are, for their primary qualities, is just another set of appearances, for example, the appearances of things in the scientific experiments on the basis of which we reduce colours to light-wave properties etc. Contrary to what the objection supposes, there is in fact no exit from the circle of appearances. Put differently, there is no way of eliminating the knower from the known, no way of achieving a view of the world which is not the view of someone. It is no accident and no surprise, consequently, that historically those philosophers who wanted to deny the possibility of rationalist Metaphysics were preoccupied with questions in the theory of knowledge or epistemology, the next division of Philosophy which I shall consider.

2.3 Epistemology or The Theory of Knowledge

For several centuries and still in the thinking of some Philosophers, the Theory of Knowledge (Epistemology) is the heart of Philosophy. Epistemology is concerned with such questions as, What can we know? How can we know? Can we ever know anything for certain? Does all our knowledge have foundations in something certain? What might such foundations be? What are the differences between knowledge and belief, and how are they related? It is the questions about foundations for knowledge which I shall illustrate here, since the search for secure foundations for knowledge characterized the main movements in philosophy from the seventeenth to the early twentieth century. The search was something both philosophers known as rationalists and philosophers known as empiricists had in common, and makes possible their comparison.

One of the founders of modern philosophy, Descartes, who is usually classed as a rationalist (believing in the role of human reason in the construction of knowledge), was centrally concerned to find a secure foundation for all knowledge, something that would be beyond doubt, something certain. In the course of his enquiries, he tells us, he found that he could doubt everything he had hitherto believed, but not his own existence. Indeed, to doubt this own existence was immediately self-refuting, for only a doubter who exists can doubt. Hence, his famous conclusion, 'Cogito ergo sum' (often translated, 'I think therefore I am'). Or as Descartes himself puts the argument in the *Discourse on the Method of Rightly Directing One's Reason and of seeking Truth in the Sciences*:

. . . in conduct one sometimes has to follow opinions that one knows to be most uncertain just as if they were indubitable; but since my present aim was to give myself up to the pursuit of truth alone, I thought I must do the very opposite, and reject as if absolutely false anything as to which I could imagine the least doubt, in order to see if I should not be left at the end believing something that was absolutely indubitable. So, because our senses sometimes deceive us, I chose to suppose that nothing was such as they lead us to imagine. Because there are men who make mistakes in reasoning even as regards the simplest points of geometry and perpetrate fallacies, and seeing that I was as liable to error as anyone else, I rejected as false all the arguments I had so far taken for demonstrations. Finally, considering that the very same experiences as we have in waking life may occur also while asleep, without there being at that time any truth in them, I decided to feign that everything that had entered my head hitherto was no more than the illusion of dreams. But immediately upon this, I noticed that while I was trying to think everything false, it must needs be that I, who was thinking this, was something. And observing that this truth, 'I am thinking, therefore I exist' was so solid and secure that the most extravagant suppositions of the sceptics could not overthrow it, I judged that I need not scruple to accept it as the first principle of philosophy that I was seeking.

In this passage, Descartes follows out a method of systematic doubt and arrives at a belief which he cannot doubt without self-contradiction. He proceeds to take this as the first principle or foundation of all his knowledge, and shortly afterwards puts to work what he has discovered:

After this I considered in general what is requisite to the truth and certainty of a proposition; for since I had just found one that I knew to have this nature, I thought I must also know what this certainty consists in. Observing that there is nothing at all in the statement 'I am thinking therefore I exist' which assures me that I speak the truth, except that I see very clearly that in order to think I must exist, I judged that I could take it as a general rule that whatever we conceive very clearly and distinctly is true.

These passages from Descartes show some characteristic features of a long tradition of epistemologically oriented philosophy. Descartes' procedure is introspective; he relies on what is subjectively evident to him; he does not consider what difference it might make that he is doing his thinking in a language which is public, shared by others and which pre-exists his thinking. All these characteristics are shared by both rationalist and empiricist philosophies, and all have been challenged in the present century, as I shall shortly consider. But before I do so, I must say a little about empiricism.

Whereas Descartes seeks to bootstrap himself to knowledge by (re-)constructing it from his own certainty in his own existence, empiricist philosophers looked to our sense experience – and, primarily, to what we visually experience – as providing the foundations on which our knowledge can be (re-)constructed. Whereas Descartes elsewhere in his philosophy took certain of our ideas to be innate (another element in his rationalism) empiricists have always argued that there is nothing in the mind which is not connected in some way to sense experience. Of course, sense experience is always only experience of how something appears to us, but for empiricists the important thing about appearances is that they are certain and thus provide secure foundations for knowledge. For though we can doubt that something which now appears to me blue or round really is blue or round, we cannot (it seems) doubt that it now really appears to me blue or round. We might have doubts about whether the word 'blue' applies to this colour or the word 'round' to this shape, but this is the only kind of doubt possible and verbal error the only possible kind of error.

The most important empiricist philosophers were Locke, Berkeley, Hume and, in this century, Bertrand Russell (1872–1970), Rudolf Carnap (1891–1970) and A.J. Ayer.

What has become generally accepted, even by empiricists, is that the project of building up all our knowledge from statements about experience ('observation sentences' in the influential version of the Logical Positivists, of whom Carnap was the most important) cannot be carried out: the things we think we know just do not relate to experience in the ways empiricists have imagined nor can we find a satisfactory way of expressing what it is that is supposedly indubitable in experience. The work of the American Philosopher, W.V.O. Quine, has been particularly influential in undermining the credibility of traditional empiricism; I shall have more to say about Quine later on. But rather than charting the fall of empiricism here, I want rather to say something about some general objections which apply to both the rationalist and empiricist programmes in Epistemology.

Epistemology has always been subjective and individualistic in its approach, as well as preoccupied with foundations. Its characteristic questions have the form, 'How do I know that *p*?' (where the '*p*' means any proposition). A common answer has been, 'When I have a justified true belief that *p*'. Rationalists and empiricists disagree over what truth is and what justifies a belief, but they are both happy with this way of approaching questions about knowledge. There have been philosophers in the past who have tried to see things differently, notably Hegel. But in the present century, it is probably Wittgenstein who has done most, at least in the world of Anglo-American Philosophy to challenge the ruling assumptions of the whole field of Epistemology. For Wittgenstein – or, at least, many readings of Wittgenstein – urges us to see our knowledge as something public, social and as having a history, not as something private, individual and out of time. As opposed to Descartes' 'I think therefore I am', Wittgenstein might be thought of as holding that 'I am because we are'. In particular, we cannot but articulate our knowledge in language and this characteristically (or, on a stronger view, necessarily) comes to us as a public, social and historical product. To this, Quine would add that knowledge does not have foundations but rather is like a ship at sea, always afloat when we encounter it. We can reconstruct it plank by plank but never all at once.

These themes from Wittgenstein and Quine are also major

themes in the Philosophy of Science, to which I now turn, and, indeed, many Philosophers would see philosophy of science as the heir to old-style Epistemology. Certainly, I for one find books on the philosophy of science invariably more provocative to thinking about knowledge than anything currently on offer in Epistemology.

2.4 Philosophy of Science

Whereas Epistemology is concerned with the nature of knowledge and belief in general, Philosophy of Science is concerned with the nature of scientific knowledge: How are scientific laws related to observation and experiment? How, if it does, does scientific knowledge accumulate and progress? What are the differences, if any, between the knowledge produced in the natural sciences, the social sciences and the humanities? How do scientific theories have practical implications? And so on.

One leading view in the Philosophy of Science, associated with the name of Sir Karl Popper, holds that scientific knowledge progresses by means of successive conjectures and refutations. Scientists do not and cannot build up theories purely from observation and experiment, since the data of observation and experiment are not self-interpreting: where one scientist sees dephlogisticated air, another sees oxygen. Rather, scientists must make a best guess – a conjecture, a hypothesis, a theory – about the way the world is, and then test this as well as they are able by controlled observation and experiment. But such testing can never conclusively prove a conjecture. It may be, for example, that we conjecture that all pandas are herbivorous and we may observe more and more herbivorous pandas. But, it has long been argued, this does not and cannot rule out the possibility that the next panda born tomorrow will be carnivorous: this is what, following Hume, is called 'the problem of induction' from observed to not (yet) observed instances. Popper accepts the terms of this problem of induction but argues that the lesson we should draw from it is that it is pointless to seek more and more instances which support a conjecture of ours. The rational thing to do – and the thing rational scientists do, according to Popper – is to look for instances which would falsify the conjecture. Having conjectured that 'All A's are B', don't continue to look for A's which *are* B, but look for A's which are *not* B. According to Popper, science consists of all those of our conjectures which are so formulated that they could be falsified by counter-instances, and conjectures are rationally acceptable (believable) to the extent that they have withstood attempts to falsify them.

This doctrine of falsificationism has the advantage that it avoids the insuperable problems which attach to any view of science which sees science as either concerned with generalizing from data (induction) or with proving hypotheses. It also recognizes the historical dimension of science: new conjectures are built on the basis of old ones, both those which have been falsified and those which have so far not been. But falsification has its own problems, notably that it does not seem to correspond to the way scientists actually work. Scientists are the last people to try to falsify their own conjectures; they tend rather to defend them with any supporting evidence that they can lay their hands on, and often enough actually in the face of counter-evidence. Either science is not a progressive and cumulative enterprise, in which each generation of scientists builds on the work of the last, or the doctrine of falsificationism is wrong, or – possibly – both.

Strong support for the idea that science is not cumulative, at least not in the straightforward way we usually assume, has come from studies in the history of science – studies to which Philosophers have paid increasing attention. If you look at the sciences over long periods of time, they are marked by periodic revolutions in approach, usually associated with the work of one great figure – for example, Newton and Einstein, associated with two great revolutions in physics. When a revolution occurs, it seems that scientists before and after not only have radically different ideas about the way the world is – whether it is flat or round, whether the sun goes round the earth or the earth round the sun – but are actually concerned with different questions and with different parts of reality. This view is argued forcefully in Thomas Kuhn's *The Structure of Scientific Revolutions* (1962), a book which has had an impact on contemporary Philosophy of Science only equalled by Popper's own *Logic of Scientific Discovery* (1934; not translated into English until 1959). This impact has occurred because Philosophers have read Kuhn as casting a great deal of sceptical doubt on our ordinary beliefs about scientific progress and the accumulation of knowledge. Kuhn has been read as providing historical evidence from the practice of science for philosophical doctrines of *relativism* about knowledge.

Relativism is not just one but really a family of related doctrines which, put crudely, deny that there are any 'absolute' or 'final' truths and assert that what we call truth is always relative to something or other: to our interests, to background assumptions which could be other than what they are, to frameworks of thinking, to our culture and values, and so on. Some such views have often appealed to anthropologists, impressed by how different from one another cultures are and with the impossibility (or undesirability) of judging the fundamental beliefs of a culture true or false and, hence, desirable or undesirable. Kuhn's book has been enthusiastically read by anthropologists and, indeed, by social scientists in general and Philosophers who take a special interest in the character of the social sciences. There are other reasons for this enthusiasm, apart from reluctance to judge the worlds of other peoples.

Notably, there is a quite commonsensical view, which social scientists have greatly developed, which sees the character of social reality as being radically different from that of the natural world. In particular, this view has it that atoms and molecules, gravitational and magnetic fields, tigers and lemons, and so on and so forth, exist as they are quite independently of our conceptions of them. But, in contrast, social objects are held to be what they are at least in part in virtue of the way we conceive them. Marriages, for example, do not exist independently of human thinking, since marriages can only take place through the performance of actions which we endow with a certain meaning, to which we give a certain conceptualization. In the social world, nothing can happen but thinking makes it so, and thinking (it may appear) can make it any way it chooses. There is no 'true' or 'essential' or 'real' marriage waiting to be discovered by a guru or a government committee. The idea and institution of marriage is invented, not discovered. When anthropologists study the marriage practices of other societies, what they are calling 'marriage' is really that set of practices which appear most analogous to ours in the part they play in that other society to the part played by marriage in ours. It is similarity of function which makes translation and comparison possible; nonetheless, what marriage *is* in different societies is really different to the extent that it is differently conceived. Indeed, anthropologists will say that it is often the case that the analogy between another culture's practices and ours is weak or non-existent, so that the anthropologist is hard put to translate their practices into terms meaningful to us. In exactly similar terms, the historian may report that things were very different in other times and places, so that, for example, ethics for the Ancient Greeks was a set of ideas and practices radically different from what *morality* is for us. At the limit, the anthropologist or the historian may feel that the inhabitants of the other culture live in another world and that their culture cannot satisfactorily be translated or interpreted to us. The only possible way to under-stand the culture and bridge the gap which relativism identifies is to try to join it – the kind of thing Carlos Castaneda reports attempting in books such as *The Teachings of Don Juan* (1970).

Interestingly, Kuhn came to similar or identical conclusions to those reached by relativistically inclined anthropologists: after a scientific revolution, Kuhn said, scientists 'live in another world'. Often enough, too, the older generation of scientists is never able to see the world in the new ways required by the new science which emerges from the revolution. Science is then only able to change because old scientists die and new ones take their place. To use a common technical term of the literature which discusses these issues, old and new views are *incommensurable* – they cannot be rationally compared with or translated into each other; they can only be experienced as different lived worlds. The parallel with the anthropologists' views is exact and both positions are thoroughly relativistic.

Of course, by no means all Philosophers want to embrace such relativistic conclusions; probably the majority of those concerned with such issues are busy trying to refute relativist arguments. They ask such awkward questions as this: Is a claim such as 'Truth is always relative' supposed to be true only relatively or absolutely? – and, if the latter, Isn't it incon-sistent to believe as absolutely true the claim that truth is always relative? Anti-relativists also contest the claim that

cultures can construct their worlds in radically incommensurable ways. Is it really possible for another culture to operate a
different conception of logic or rationality from our own?

Such questions are the subject of lively debate in the
Philosophy of Science, both as it concerns social science and as
it concerns natural science. The debate is carried on in real
dialogue with practising social and natural scientists and I
think that for students, study of questions in the philosophy of
science is often a particularly rewarding part of their courses,
since the answers you reach really do seem to make a difference
to the way you think about your world. Philosophy of Science
has also been enriched by the happy fact that many of the
leading contributors to recent debates have been gifted writers
and polemicists. This is true, for example, of such figures as
Paul Feyerabend, Ernest Gellner, Ian Hacking and Imre
Lakatos (1920–70). However, it is also the case that in-depth
pursuit of many of the most interesting questions in the
Philosophy of Science involves coming to terms with topics in
the often difficult and abstruse field of the Philosophy of
Language, where the prose is often heavy going.

2.5 Philosophy of Language

For many Philosophers, Philosophy of Language is today the
heart of their subject in a way that a hundred or even fifty years
ago Epistemology was central. That is not to say that they all
see it as important for the same reasons, or agree on what the
central questions of the Philosophy of Language are. For some
Philosophers, all Philosophy is Philosophy of Language
insofar as it is, or ought to be, the study of meanings or concepts as articulated in language. A variety of such approaches
to Philosophy have existed, variously called 'analysis', 'lin-
guistic philosophy' and 'ordinary language philosophy' –
approaches which were dominant in British universities until
the 1960s. For other Philosophers, Philosophy of Language is
central simply because so much of our experience and knowledge of the world is mediated by, expressed in or even constituted by, language. For others still, Philosophy of Language
is about analysing the language in which we talk about
language itself, about 'meaning', 'sentence', 'statement', 'proposition' and so on. Finally (and these positions are certainly

not mutually exclusive), Philosophy of Language is seen as an activity of theorizing about the ways in which language relates to the mind and to the world. In this section, I cannot hope to do more than give a few examples and convey a little of the flavour of the enormous range of discussion in contemporary Philosophy of Language.

To begin with, recall the discussion of the previous section where I talked of problems of translation and interpretation of another culture's language and practices. In his book *Word and Object* (1960), W.V.O. Quine set out to show just how far-reaching are such problems of understanding another culture, and specifically another language, by means of an invented anthropological example, which every Philosophy student now becomes familiar with. Imagine, says Quine, that you are an anthropologist trying to translate the language of a hitherto isolated tribe. No bilingual informants exist and you have to work directly with people whose language you do not share and who do not share your language either. You somehow establish a working relationship with a tribesman in which you point to things and he names them. For example, a rabbit appears and he says 'gavagai' when you point at it. You may think that 'gavagai' means 'rabbit', and your confidence in this translation will increase with repeated correlations between your pointing to a rabbit and your informant saying 'gavagai'. But can you be sure that your translation is the right one? After all, whenever a rabbit appears, so too do parts of a rabbit undetached from its body – heads and legs, for example. Couldn't 'gavagai' actually mean 'undetached rabbit part'? Again, isn't it to beg a lot of questions simply to assume that the tribesman has the same conception of permanent objects as we do. When he says 'Gavagai', perhaps he means 'It's rabbiting', rather as we say 'It's raining'. There have indeed been many anthropologists, notably the American anthropological linguist, Benjamin Lee Whorf (1897–1941), who have claimed that other cultures do have different conceptions of objects from our own.

One of the conclusions which Quine draws from his invented example is that when engaging in what has come to be called 'radical translation', we can never be sure that we have hit on the right translation. The relation between the evidence (the tribesman's behaviour, and so on) and the conclusion (the translation) is like the relation between evidence and a theory: the theory is *underdetermined* by the evidence, and represents a conjecture which goes beyond the information given. One possible response to this is to grant that translations, like theories, are underdetermined by the evidence which is used to support them, but to argue that many conceivable translations can simply be ruled out as candidates for being correct on the grounds that they would imply that the human mind works in ways which we know it does not work in. The human mind is so constructed that the categories it naturally constructs would never include a monstrosity such as 'undetached rabbit part'. This response is basically that made to Quine by the linguist, Noam Chomsky. Because Chomsky answers Quine's scepticism by appealing to human nature, his position is a naturalistic one, and naturalism of this sort is currently quite influential in several branches of Philosophy, as I noted previously.

Many other questions in the Philosophy of Language can arise from exploration of Quine's apparently simple example. For example, when we talk about 'what the tribesman means by "gavagai" ', what do *we* mean by this talk of someone meaning something? What is the meaning of 'meaning'? One answer (particularly associated with the name of the Philosopher H.P. Grice) is to say that the idea of what someone means by something is to be analysed in terms of what they intend: the *tribesman* means 'rabbit' by 'gavagai' just because he intends to pick out a rabbit by using 'gavagai'. When we say, in a different vein, that 'gavagai' means 'rabbit', this is really only a roundabout way of saying that 'gavagai' is that word all the tribe use when they intend to refer to a rabbit. What we might call the tribe's convention of calling rabbits 'gavagai' is analysed in terms of the intentions speakers have. On Grice's approach, intention is a more basic concept than meaning or convention, because meaning and convention are analysed in terms of it, but not vice versa: meaning and convention are *reduced* to intention. Any analysis of meaning in terms of intention makes out meaning to be 'something in the head' – meaning arises from mental activity, from what Philosophers call *intentionality*, the directedness of the mind on the world. On this approach, Philosophy of Language is obviously connected to Philosophy of Mind.

But the intentionalist approach is not the only one in contemporary Philosophy of Language, nor is it the dominant one. There is also a set of traditions, beginning with the pioneering work of the German logician, Gottlob Frege (1848–1925), which are committed to detaching the idea of meaning from ideas about the mind on the basis of the belief that while every mind is different, meanings surely have to be the same if communication by means of language is to be possible. There are several ways of trying to achieve the goal of detaching meaning from mind. One involves treating meanings as senses of words which are in some way abstract and not mind-dependent, rather as in arithmetic the numbers represented by number-names are thought of as existing independently and autonomously of our thinking about them. Another way involves treating meanings as belonging first of all to sentences rather than individual words, and arguing that the meaning of a sentence is given by the conditions under which an utterance of the sentence would be *true*. On this approach, 'gavagai' would mean 'rabbit' if and only if the real-world conditions under which an utterance of 'Rabbit!' is true are identical to the conditions under which 'Gavagai!' is true (where '!' here means that the utterance is an assertion). In this analysis, there is no reference to anything in anyone's head but simply the establishing of a correlation between what is said and the way things are. (In fact, as I have presented it, what is in the speakers' heads could be quite different from head to head.)

The approach to the analysis of meaning in terms of the analysis of truth is generally known as *truth-conditional semantics*. In contemporary Philosophy, the approach is particularly associated with the name of the American Philosopher, Donald Davidson. Work in truth-conditional semantics is closely linked to current work in logic and linguistics and the work has generated a large, technical literature which undergraduate students will certainly encounter.

There are still other ways of thinking about meaning, some of which arise from an important range of arguments and examples designed to show that meaning *cannot* be something mental, something in the head. The arguments were first developed in the later work of Ludwig Wittgenstein, whose posthumous book *Philosophical Investigations* (1953) is a key text in virtually all Philosophy courses, despite the fact of its considerable obscurity. Much clearer presentations of related arguments, and some telling examples, are to be found in current American Philosophy, and I shall in fact illustrate the general argument with an example drawn from an influential paper by Tyler Burge, 'Individualism and the Mental' (1978). Burge asks us to imagine a man who has arthritis in the hip and knee waking up one morning with a pain in his thigh. He goes to his doctor and reports, 'Doctor, the arthritis has spread to my thigh'. The doctor replies, 'No, it hasn't. Arthritis is a disease of the joints'. Burge now asks: what did the patient mean by the word 'arthritis' when he said that the arthritis had spread to his thigh? Specifically, did he have a different concept of arthritis from the doctor, call it a concept of *tharthritis* (a disease of the joints and thighs)? Burge answers that as used by the patient, 'arthritis' did not, in fact, mean anything different from what it meant to the doctor. Consequently, the meaning of 'arthritis' is not in the patient's head, since what is in his head is inconsistent with the meaning of arthritis (he *thinks* you can have arthritis in the thigh, and he doesn't think the thigh is a joint). On Burge's view, the meaning of 'arthritis' is not in *anyone's* head, but rather exists *between* the members of the community of which the patient is a part. When the patient uses the word 'arthritis', he invokes its meaning in the community, almost as if he was using the word in quotation marks; he does not invoke or refer to any private meaning in his head – and Burge, like Wittgenstein before him, would go further and say he *cannot*, for reasons I do not have space to expound here. Clearly, however, there is *something* apparently in the patient's head, namely his false belief that arthritis has spread to his thigh. If we now wished to ask what a belief is, we would have to move on from the Philosophy of Language and into the Philosophy of Mind.

2.6 Philosophy of Mind

Under the heading of Philosophy of Mind are considered such central questions of Philosophy as, What is the relationship between mind and body? What is the nature of the self? Do we have free-will? and What is the character of such mental phenomena as desire, emotion, will and belief? Interestingly, the way in which, over the centuries, these questions have been approached by philosophers (and psychologists) has generally shown the influence of the successful, prestigious sciences of the time. So, for example, Hume modelled his account of the inner world of the mind on a Newtonian view of the working of the external world. Ideas in the mind are analogous to atoms of matter in motion, essentially independent but connected by what later come to be thought of in psychology as 'laws of association'. In the first half of our own century, when natural science was strongly oriented to verifiable observation, the internal laws of association were turned outwards and became the stimulus–response patterns of behaviourist psychology.

At the present time, the mind is increasingly thought of – by Philosophers, psychologists and the lay public – by analogy with the computer. So it is said, for example, that minds relate to bodies as computer software relates to computer hardware; mental processes are compared to the running of programs, that is, to operations with and on symbols or representations. The idea of belief or a belief – say, the belief that p – could be explicated in terms of the computer analogy as involving a computational relation to a symbolic representation of p. Having the belief that p leads one to operate on and with p, to produce particular kinds of inference and behaviour which could be simulated or, on a stronger view, reproduced in the symbol-manipulations of a computer program.

How good is the analogy between the mind and computer programs? How like a human mind could we make a computer program? These are questions which currently attract a good deal of attention in the Philosophy of Mind. One Philosopher, John Searle, is extremely doubtful both about the mind–computer program analogy and the project of artificial intelligence to build mind-like computer programs. He presents his doubts by means of a simple example, the so-called Chinese Room, which like Quine's 'gavagai' example is one which will become familiar to every student. So here it is. (You can also find it, accessibly, in Searle's 1984 Reith Lectures, *Minds, Brains and Science*).

Imagine, says Searle, that I am locked in a room into which are passed batches of Chinese writing (Searle doesn't read Chinese) together with rules in English (he reads English) which allow him to correlate bits of Chinese writing across the different batches. This is sufficient for him to receive material in Chinese and, to outsiders, appear to answer – in Chinese – questions about it. But does Searle *understand* Chinese in all this? Not a bit of it, says Searle; I merely co-ordinate one bit of Chinese which I don't understand (it may be a question) with another bit of Chinese (it may be an answer) which I don't understand either. But I do produce an *appearance* of understanding, and in this I am just like a sophisticated computer program. For a sophisticated computer program does not (and, Searle argues, cannot) do anything more than Searle does in the Chinese room. A computer program simply manipulates symbols which have no meaning for it. Its symbols acquire meaning by being assigned meaning by those human beings who use the program; the symbols have no more intrinsic meaning for the computer program than Chinese has for Searle. As with the computer program, so with the Chinese room: all the meaning is outside it. However much you complicate the picture, symbol crunching can never yield understanding. Hence, you cannot reproduce the human mind in a computer (the goal of advocates of a 'strong' artificial intelligence approach). Equally, you cannot hope to understand human minds through the computer analogy. For what Searle says about understanding generalizes to other phenomena, such as belief: treating a belief as a relation to or operations on a symbolic representation will always leave something out. But what?

Though Searle sitting in his Chinese room is a person or self, what goes on in the Chinese room makes no connection with that person or self; this is what it means to say that Searle doesn't understand the Chinese text he is processing. In the case of the computer, more radically, there simply is no person or self inside it with which the symbol manipulation could connect. This is what is missing from it. Understanding and belief are attributes of persons or selves, not of minds, bodies or brains. No person or self – no understanding or belief. So what is missing from the computer is any analogue of the person or self which is the subject of understanding, belief and all the other commonsense mental states and processes. But what is a person or self or subject?

This is a question which has always baffled philosophers. Hume's expression of his bafflement is famous; looking into himself he never can find just a self but always something else:

> For my part, when I enter most intimately into what I call *myself*, I always stumble on some particular perception or other, of heat or cold, light or shade, love or hatred, pain or pleasure. I never can catch *myself* at any time without a perception, and never can observe any thing but the perception. (*Treatise of Human Nature*)

Treatments of the self resolve themselves into two classes: those which argue or end up with the view that our concept of self or person is primitive or irreducible – we just have a sense of our own self, and that is really all that can be said – and those which seek to reduce the self to something else: a conjunction of mental states (in Hume), a brain, a body or a social construct. Much of the literature explores the issues through consideration of the question of personal identity – What makes it the case that I am me? – frequently using bizarre examples of brain transplants and disembodiment to tease out what is central to our sense of identity and, hence, of self. Other parts of the literature try to say something more than Hume manages about our sense of self, exploring the area phenomenologically, that is, in terms of how things appear to us. It is here that emphasis is often laid on our sense of ourselves as agents in the world which seems very much connected to our sense of self, for if (as in various kinds of mental illness) we lose a sense of agency, we also lose a sense of self (and vice versa). However, one of the problems with our sense of agency – our sense that we are able to decide to act and act in certain ways in the world – is that it bumps up against other common beliefs about the nature of the world, for example, the belief that everything has a cause. It is here that the philosophical problem of free-will is situated, a problem historically as intractable as that of the self.

For consider. When we think of ourselves acting of our own free-will, we think that we could have acted otherwise had we so chosen. In contrast, when we think of events in the world as causally connected, we think that given the state of affairs A obtaining at any one time, it has to be the case that B will follow, and the occurrence of B is causally explicable in the light of its antecedents. If this were not the case, B would be an unpredictable chance or random event. But then we seem to face a dilemma: either we must say that some action (say, B) of mine is sufficiently explained by its antecedents (say, A) – in which case I seem to be mistaken in thinking that I could have acted otherwise – or else my action was chance or random, in which case there is no reason why my actions should form any coherent pattern or relate intelligibly to the rest of my life and so on and so forth. Faced with dilemmas like this, philosophers have historically sought one of three ways out. First, the more tough-minded have simply argued that our belief in free-will is a delusion, and that all our actions are causally determined by their antecedents, just like all other events in the world. By controlling the antecedents, we can control the actions and so, for example, the psychologist can set up as the engineer of human souls – the position adopted by B.F. Skinner in such books as *Beyond Freedom and Dignity* (1972). Second, philosophers have denied the doctrine of universal causality, claiming that our free actions are genuinely uncaused, whilst seeking to deny that they are chance or random. Existentialists from Kierkegaard (1813–55) to Sartre have explored something like this path. Third, and this is probably the commonest position, philosophers have sought to reconcile our belief in the causal order with our belief in free-will by such means, for example, as the argument that our reasons for action are the causes of them. Daniel Dennett's highly readable *Elbow Room* (1984) is the latest in a long series of works which take such a reconciliationist line. All three positions clearly connect Philosophy of Mind to Moral Philosophy, the next sub-branch of Philosophy I shall consider. In general, the topic of free will is one which usually appeals to students because of its evident connection both to our everyday ways of thinking about ourselves and to our moral and political beliefs about how we should relate, individually and institutionally, to others.

2.7 Moral Philosophy or Ethics

To many philosophers, that we should have free will has seemed a necessary condition of any justified use of the everyday language of morals. For how could we fairly or legitimately praise or blame people for their actions, characterizing them as good or bad, virtuous or wicked, unless people were the freely responsible authors of their own actions? More pointedly, how could we justly punish anyone for wrongdoing unless the person punished did commit their crimes of their own free will? If someone was just the victim of a set of circumstances, external (social) or internal (psychological) that made it inevitable that they should have done as they did, then though it might be necessary to isolate that person from society for the good of others, it could not be right to punish them – that is, deliberately inflict some harm or loss upon them. Indeed, though we might think that what we were doing was to punish the offender, in the absence of free will we would actually be practising some form of cruelty on them, which might affect their behaviour for the better by making them averse to wrongdoing but which could not be justified as a morally justified response to a morally culpable act.

Moral Philosophy necessarily involves sorting out some view on free-will and the implications of that view for moral practices. Equally, Moral Philosophy is concerned at its centre with the classification of actions into good and bad. Where do such classifications come from? And, since people so obviously disagree in their classifications of good and bad, right and wrong, is it possible to make out a case for preferring any one classification to another? More generally, what is the nature of moral judgement and moral argument?

Consider first the question of moral judgement. If someone says 'Abortion is wrong', what sort of judgement are they making? For example, how, if at all, does saying 'Abortion is wrong' differ from saying 'I dislike abortion'? Some Philosophers have denied that there is any significant difference: to say something is wrong is just a particularly emphatic way of expressing your dislike for it. Such an emotive view of moral judgements has been endorsed by many Philosophers during this century, including the Logical Positivists of the 1920s and 1930s whose doctrines were popularized in Britain by A.J. Ayer in a famous book, *Language, Truth and Logic* (1936). One advantage of the emotive view is that it becomes easy to understand why moral judgements are so diverse and conflicting, for if moral judgements are really no more than expressions of likes and dislikes, there is really no reason why they should be any more uniform than our likes and dislikes in food and (emotivists would add) art.

It is hardly surprising that numerous arguments have been deployed against a view so threatening to our usual assumptions about the character of our moral judgements – which we typically believe to possess a certain objectivity – and which some have seen as threatening the very possibility of morality itself. One response to emotivism, and in fact a standard philosophical manoeuvre, is to point out that there is no contradiction in saying things like, 'X is wrong, but I like it' (where 'X' may be something like eating meat or beating up supporters of the rival football team) and, consequently, such terms as 'right' and 'wrong' cannot literally mean the same as 'I like', 'I dislike'. The emotivist can get round this objection by arguing that the person who says 'X is wrong, but I like it' is simply referring to some external system of morality which he or she endorses. The question then becomes whether anything underpins that external system other than the likes and dislikes of those responsible for it.

Second, an objector to emotivism is likely to point out that to say I like or dislike something does not imply that the person I am addressing should like or dislike that thing too, or that I am going to think any the worse of them if they do not share my tastes. If 'Abortion is wrong' really meant no more than 'I dislike abortion', it should have no more practical consequences than 'I dislike cabbage'. But clearly it does. People who say 'Abortion is wrong' and mean what they say not only commit themselves to avoiding having or performing an abortion, but equally commit themselves to dissuading others from participation in abortion, and thinking the worse of people who do have or perform abortions. Such a person may well want to criminalize abortion. The general idea underlying this objection might be put like this: we can only make a properly moral judgement of something when we are willing to imply that if it's wrong (right) for you, it's wrong (right) for me and that if it's wrong (right) for me, it's wrong (right) for you, unless there is some relevant difference between us. Put technically, this is the thesis – made central to moral philosophy by Kant – that moral judgements are and must be *universalizable*. The problem at this point, and one which the emotivist is willing to exploit, is to know whether universalizability is a feature of the *logic* of moral judgements, from which there is no escape, or whether it is, in fact, a disguised and partisan piece of moralizing which we are free to reject. On the other hand, the emotivists' own re-analysis of universalizability may sound distinctly lame to you; they accept that there is a difference between saying 'Abortion is wrong' and 'I dislike abortion' but that it amounts to this: the person who says 'Abortion is wrong' is expressing a dislike of abortion *and* also urging or commanding others to do likewise. So, they say the correct analysis of 'Abortion is wrong' is this: 'I dislike abortion. Do so as well!' This is supposed to differentiate this case from cases of taste, since when I say 'I dislike cabbage' I don't imply 'Do so as well!'

This is not the end to objections to emotivism, and it is worth considering a third line of objection. Here the objector points out that if you ask someone why they dislike cabbage, it is a perfectly adequate answer to say 'I just do'. You don't *have* to have any reasons for disliking cabbage; it can be simply a matter of taste. In contrast, if when asked why they thought abortion wrong, someone answered 'I just think it is', we would (I think) have a strong sense that this isn't good enough. For we expect people to be able to furnish *reasons* for their moral judgements, where a reason is something we in turn are obliged either to accept (as a good reason) or reject (as a bad one). So if someone asked why they think abortion wrong, responds 'Because it is a form of murder, and murder is wrong', we now know *why* they think abortion is wrong and also *how* to continue the argument: we either have to deny that the killing of a foetus is (always) unjustified – hence not a form of murder – or else deny that the foetus is the sort of thing that can be murdered. In all probability, we will end up arguing over what it is to be a person or human being and how and when something becomes one.

In introducing this third argument against the emotivist view, I have moved from talking about moral judgement to considering moral argument. But once again, the emotivist can come back with some kind of rejoinder. Here the emotivist might say something like this. Consider how, when asked why I dislike cabbage, I might say not simply 'I just do' but something like 'Because of the taste' or 'Because of the smell'. These look like reasons; they indicate what it is about cabbage that I dislike. But pressed again to answer why I dislike the taste or the smell, I may have nothing more to say than something like

'I just find it awful'. My reasons for disliking cabbage inevitably run out and in the end I can only express a reaction or an attitude. The emotivist now asks: Is it, in the end, any different with moral argument? Won't the opponent of abortion end up having to say something like 'Well, it just seems to me that the embryo is already a human life'? And isn't that not the statement of a reason, but an expression of a way of seeing or a way of experiencing the world – an expression of something subjective with which we are not and cannot be obliged to agree or disagree, but about which we can merely indicate whether or not we see or experience things the same way. In other words, though moral argument can delay the time at which we simply have to express the way we respond to the world, it can never eliminate the ultimate dependence of a moral viewpoint on such subjective response. And isn't this all the emotivist needs to vindicate the position initially articulated?

Many contemporary Philosophers do indeed find themselves driven back into a position which concedes the major emotivist claims, even against their own wishes and certainly in defiance of what commonsense assumes about the objectivity of moral judgement and argument. At least one contemporary Philosopher, Alasdair MacIntyre, in his book *After Virtue* (1980) tries to reinterpret the predicament of moral philosophy in historical terms: the loss of the possibility of moral certainty is historically explicable. Other Philosophers are inclined to fall back on a positive theory of human nature as a way of exiting from the corner into which emotivism has forced them. For consider, the problems the emotivist has created can be construed as yet another instance of philosophical scepticism: faced with the remorseless questions of the sceptic (here, the emotivist), we find ourselves ultimately unable to give reasons for something – here the idea that moral judgements are other or more than the expression of our subjective experiences and responses – we thought we had reason for believing. And one response to scepticism is to upgrade our evaluation of the 'primitive' responses and experiences we are obliged to fall back on. It is not a *defect* in morality that, in the end, it depends on subjective experience and response, especially if (contrary to a too-easy assumption) these subjective phenomena evidence common ways of experiencing and responding – for example, a common sympathetic response to the suffering of others. It is because such common or shared responses exist that, despite everything, moral argument remains possible and sometimes fruitful.

I suspect most people will find this variety of philosophical naturalism naively optimistic; it just does not square with the fact of irreconcilable moral differences. Faced with these, some will say, we had better look for some other means than morality as the way of organizing a common life together. But what? In the remainder of this section I want to say something about self-interest in its relation to morality, especially because self-interest is generally presented to us and thought of as incompatible with and opposed to any moral point of view on things. Isn't morality all about seeing things impartially and independently of one's own interests? This is certainly what Kant thought; as H.J. Paton expresses Kant's idea, 'The attempt to stand outside our personal maxims and estimate impartially and impersonally their fitness to be principles of action for others than ourselves is a necessary condition of all moral judgement.' In addition, one might wonder how self-interest could ever bring people together; surely it is self-interest which divides people and only morality which can bring them together? But then one might ask, why should anyone be moral if it is not in their own self-interest? These kinds of question can be explored and illuminated, I believe, by means of a fascinating and widely discussed paradox in self-interested action, always illustrated in the literature with the now famous example of the Prisoners' Dilemma.

Two men are held prisoner, separately and in isolation, but each charged with a joint offence. Each is told that if the charge is not proved, they will each go free, and that the only evidence against them may be their own confession. They are also told that if both confess to the act, they will each go to prison for one year. If one confesses and the other does not, the confessor will go free and receive a financial reward, while the non-confessor will go to prison for five years. Each is told that the other has been told exactly the same things. The question now asked is this: In such circumstances, what should each of them to do?

To see their dilemma, imagine you are one of the prisoners. If you don't confess, and your fellow-prisoner does, he goes free with a reward but you go to jail for five years. If you confess, and your fellow prisoner doesn't, the situation is reversed. If you both confess, you both go to jail. If neither of you confess, you both go free. It may seem rational not to confess. But if the other prisoner thinks you aren't going to confess, he has a motive to confess: he will go free *and* get a reward. Since you can anticipate this possibility, you have a reason to confess. In fact, you have an overriding reason to confess (and so does he) with the result that you both go to jail when both of you could have gone free. Prisoners' Dilemma is a dilemma (and the outcome paradoxical) because if each prisoner consults only his own self-interest, he will end up doing something (confessing) which makes him worse off than he could have been had he acted differently. Yet self-interested action is supposed to be that which maximizes our own individual reward.

Had the prisoners belonged to an organization which severely punished squealers, then each would have had a reason, perhaps an overriding one, to not confess and both would have gone free. Equally, were they party to something like a code of honour among thieves, then neither would have confessed and both would have gone free – a better solution, from the standpoint of self-interest, than going to jail. In other words, a code of honour – a morality – would actually have served their individual interests by preventing the prisoners from acting in a self-destructive way. Some would say that this is the *point* of morality, and that the reason for being moral is that it is in our interests to be moral. Morality is not opposed to self-interest, but serves and enlightens our pursuit of it.

Such an idea is attractive to Philosophers who think that Prisoners' Dilemma provides a model for common situations of ordinary social life, involving whole communities of people. There are many examples of such situations in Mancur Olson's *The Logic of Collective Action* (1965). It is indeed possible to read much moral and political philosophy as arguing that the problems of social life in general have the same structure as is illustrated by Prisoners' Dillemma. I shall provide some further illustrations in the course of the next sub-section, in relation to the history of Political Philosophy.

2.8 Political Philosophy or Political Theory

For Philosophers, whose sense of time is perhaps rather different from that of other academic specialists, modern political thought begins with Hobbes, from whose *Leviathan* (1651) Philosophy students always remember a famous sentence in which Hobbes describes the human condition in the absence of government, the human condition in what is generally called *a state of nature*:

In such condition, there is no place for industry; because the fruit thereof is uncertain: and consequently no culture of the earth; no navigation, nor use of the commodities that may be imported by sea; no commodious building; no instruments of moving, and removing, such things as require much force; no knowledge of the face of the earth; no account of time; no arts; no letters; no society; and which is worst of all, continual fear, and danger of violent death; and the life of man, solitary, poor, nasty, brutish and short.

For Hobbes, human beings are moved by self-interest and this makes it both possible and necessary for them to submit to political authority: necessary because self-interest is the source of their tendency to default on their obligations or promises (their 'covenants') whenever it appears to be in their interest to do so. But if everyone defaulted when it seemed to be in their interests, all would find themselves back in a state of nature and, consequently, worse off. Just as in Prisoners' Dilemma, self-interested action produces unintended ('counter-final') consequences which defeat the aims of the original action. In Hobbes's view of things, morality alone is not enough to overcome the tendency of self-interested individuals to default on their obligations; he thinks that only the prospect of punishment can deter individuals from renegade acts. As he puts, it, 'Covenants, without the swords, are but words, and of no strength to secure a man at all.'

Consequently, Hobbes argues that rational individuals have an interest in submitting themselves to strong government, in fact to a highly authoritarian, monarchical sovereign which Hobbes calls the Leviathan. Their only right against the sovereign is the right of self-preservation should the sovereign threaten their own existence: in comparison with what is argued for by other seventeenth-century philosophers, Hobbes acknowledges only this extremely limited right of rebellion.

Over a century later, another major figure in the history of
political thought, Rousseau, sought to represent the problem
of self-interested defection from the covenant or contract of
political society in a less bleak fashion, less as a simple clash of
will and force in which all that matters is that the sovereign be
strong enough to prevail over wayward subjects. So in *The
Social Contract* (1762), Rousseau links the idea of rationality
to the idea of freedom. The irrational man (and Rousseau
means man, not woman) is unfree, and so self-interested but
mutually destructive defection from what is in the common
interest is not only irrational but renders a man unfree. When
society acts to restrain or punish the defector, it can be seen as
doing nothing worse than to 'force him to be free'. In this
famous phrase, Rousseau reconciles the defence of political
society (which implies restraint) with an ideal of freedom
(which did not concern the authoritarian Hobbes). Of course,
Rousseau's solution to the dilemma of reconciling freedom
with constraint does depend on sustaining the idea that an
identifiable common interest can exist in a society. Much of the
Social Contract is given over to indicating what such a
common interest might be and how it could be found out and
expressed in what Rousseau calls 'the general will' of a society.
Rousseau is far from optimistic about ever actually sustaining
such a general will. Only in small, egalitarian societies does the
basis for it exist. Most later political theorists are even more
pessimistic than Rousseau, and it is characteristic of twentieth-
century political thought to reject the very idea that political
society can be constituted around a common interest. Rather,
it is because we *differ* fundamentally in our interests that
politics is necessary. But in the nineteenth century, the idea of
common interest continued to be accepted by thinkers as otherwise diverse as Karl Marx and John Stuart Mill.

Marx will often merit a course of his own in a Philosophy
degree, where he will be studied in conjunction with Hegel,
Engels (1820–95), Lenin (1870–1924) and other Marxist
theorists and political leaders. Marx certainly read Rousseau,
and the future communist society Marx describes in his early
writings and in *The Communist Manifesto* (1848) has much in
common with the ideal polity of *The Social Contract*. Interestingly, it has recently been argued that Marx's ideas on the
possibility of revolutionary change to bring about a socialist

and then a communist society are vulnerable to criticism from the same standpoint of a generalization of the Prisoners' Dilemma idea which I have used to present the theories of Hobbes and Rousseau. The argument (due to Mancur Olson and Allen Buchanan) goes like this. Marx says that the working class under capitalism share an interest in replacing a capitalist with a socialist organization of society; all workers will benefit from such a change. But individual workers will presumably benefit regardless of their individual contribution to bringing about such a transition and, in any case, many of the benefits will accrue to future generations not the present one. Individual contributions to bringing about a revolutionary transition necessarily involve costs: at the very least, subscriptions to trade unions and political parties; at most, loss of life in a revolutionary struggle. The self-interested worker should now reason as follows: if the revolution happens, I will benefit regardless of what I did to bring it about, since it is not feasible to withold the collective benefit of revolution from individuals. If I contribute to bringing it about, I stand to lose at least something and possibly even my life, but I will gain no more than anyone else. Consequently, it is not rational for me to join the struggle for revolutionary change. Now if every worker reasons like this, none of them will do anything and no revolution will happen, even though (on Marx's premisses) they are worse off under the existing capitalist state of affairs than they would be under socialism. This argument against Marx's optimism about revolutionary change is particularly interesting and effective precisely because Marx, like Hobbes and Rousseau before him, did see self-interest as one of the mainsprings of human action.

So too did John Stuart Mill. But Mill also had major concerns which were novel with respect to those of the political thinkers I have so far introduced, concerns which resulted in work which bears directly on issues which are still of current, practical importance. In particular, Mill – unlike Hobbes and Rousseau, certainly – was conscious of human diversity, valued it and wished to nourish it. He therefore faced, among other questions, the question of the limits of allowable diversity: what kinds of belief and behaviour should properly constituted political authority permit and what should it disallow among the citizens subject to it? Mill poses this question in his work, *On Liberty* (1859), and answers it by enunciating a fundamental principle, the subject of intense philosophical discussion in recent years:

. . . the sole end for which mankind are warranted, individually or collectively, in interfering with the action of any of their number, is self-protection. That the only purpose for which power can be rightfully exercised over any member of a civilized community, against his will, is to prevent harm to others. His own good, either physical or moral, is not a sufficient warrant.

By 'harm to others', Mill is generally understood to have meant physical or material harm of some identifiable kind. In contrast, the harm someone suffers only in virtue of beliefs they hold is not to count for purposes of determining the application of Mill's principle. Someone may be shocked, offended or disgusted by, say, homosexuality, in virtue of religious beliefs they hold, but that is no reason for the state to proscribe it. And, indeed, the liberalization in 1967 of the laws which criminalized homosexuality in Great Britain owed a great deal to a shared sense that there is an important distinction to be marked between behaviour which harms someone only because of beliefs they hold and behaviour which harms people in some sense more directly, and that legislation should only be employed, as Mill argues, to prevent harm of the latter sort. Similarly, when the question of whether pornography should be allowed to circulate has been discussed, it has generally been thought particularly relevant to determine whether it does or does not bring about identifiable harm in Mill's sense, for example, in terms of whether those exposed to or making use of pornography are as a result more or less likely to commit sexual assaults. For some recent writers, this approach has seemed too restrictive and they have challenged both the viability of any distinction between two kinds of harm as I distinguished them and the relevance or decisiveness of the harm criterion. Some feminists have argued, for example, that pornography is intrinsically degrading of women and ought to be banned on that ground alone quite independently of any consideration of more extrinsic effects.

It should be clear from these examples of homosexuality and pornography that Mill's arguments in *On Liberty* can still be the starting point for both theoretical controversy and applied argument. Such practically oriented political philosophizing is extensively practised in the USA, where the role of the Constitution and the Supreme Court in political life mean that Philosophy and Law are fairly directly entangled with each other. This is reflected in the pages of such journals as *Philosophy and Public Affairs*, a major reference point for contemporary political Philosophy, and in the work of such American Philosophers of Law as Ronald Dworkin, author of *Law's Empire* (1986).

In my next section, I look at Aesthetics or the Philosophy of Art. Though there are obvious links between art and politics, it would, I think, be misleading to try to bridge from this section to the next in the way that I have previously done. Despite the efforts of some notable contemporary Philosophers, such as Roger Scruton and Richard Wollheim, to write about aesthetic questions in ways which connect them with the mainstreams of Moral and Political Philosophy and Philosophy of Language and Mind, Aesthetics remains a small and relatively specialized sub-branch of Philosophy.

2.9 Aesthetics or the Philosophy of Art

Indeed, Aesthetics is a bit of a Cinderella, which is often enough simply left out of introductory textbooks, such as Anthony O'Hear's otherwise excellent *What Philosophy Is*. Yet in people's lives discussions and arguments about art are often enough as common and important as those to do with the morally good, the politically right or the epistemologically dubious: 'I don't think that was a very good film, do you?', 'I despise sentimental music', 'The play was just a lot of socialist rubbish', 'You can't call a load of old bricks *Art*', and so on. All such utterances provide the basis for philosophical reflection and, possibly, resolution.

In recent years, Philosophers have generally had little to say about the evaluation of art, perhaps because it has seemed obvious to them that there are no objective criteria of evaluation which compel us to agree with each other. Most Philosophers have wanted to reject the view that morality is a matter of likes and dislikes; many have been prepared to accept that artistic evaluation and preference is just that. The idea that taste is something some people have got and others haven't, so that the evaluations of the latter simply don't count seems unacceptably elitist even to Philosophers. On the other hand, reluctant as they are to admit it, most people do not treat all tastes as equal: you find it difficult to imagine how anyone not somehow deficient could possibly *like* the garish, sentimental, coy or banal picture on the greetings card they have sent you! It can't just be a matter of their having different tastes; they must surely be insensitive to what makes a picture pleasing.

But what does or ought to make a picture pleasing? On questions related to this one, philosophers have had a great deal to say. First of all, Philosophers have tried to clarify the nature of a specific interest in or attitude towards objects which they believe it is possible to adopt, the aesthetic interest or attitude. In the *Critique of Judgement* (1791), Kant developed the view which has become standard that to attend to something aesthetically is to attend to it in a disinterested, contemplative way. I can adopt such an attitude towards both the natural and the human world, including the world of Art. So, for example, when from my window I contemplate the slopes of the South Downs, without thinking whether the farmer will soon be harvesting the corn or wondering how much per acre the land is worth, and so on, then this way of seeing the Downs is aesthetic. Likewise, when I look at a painting by Cezanne without thinking of its creation, sale, subsequent history and so on, this is to look at the painting from the aesthetic standpoint. The motive for such disinterested attention to things is provided by the possibility of deriving pleasure, aesthetic pleasure, from them.

But what is this pleasure and what is it in the things attended to which produces it (when the things are beautiful) or its opposite (when the things are ugly)? Here philosophers have produced numerous, rival accounts. Simplifying a great deal, we can say that the main disagreements have been over the importance of the sensuous as opposed to the intellectual qualities of an object and, relatedly, over the respective parts played by form and content. I will say a little about each of these oppositions.

Some art affects us bodily, as with rhythmic music which makes you want to tap your feet or dance, and from this it is a short step to thinking of aesthetic pleasure as deriving from things which have the right properties to set up a range of such pleasurable bodily responses. In the nineteenth century, a physiological aesthetics was developed from just such a starting point. The trouble is that such a theory fails to do justice to the way in which such responses are dependent on a prior cognitive grasp of the structures of something, for example, the rhythmic, melodic or harmonic structures of a piece of music and, in addition, does not seem to have anything to say about, notably, the experience of drama or the novel. Watching or reading a tragedy, we have an emotional response – often enough with the physical component of tears – but this response is possible only if we understand the play or novel and is clearly informed by such understanding. Furthermore, our capacity for such strong emotional reaction to situations we know to be fictional itself seems to require an explanation which will not be couched in terms of physiology but of psychology – perhaps a theory of the unconscious. Of course, it may be that the tacit assumption I have made that a philosophical theory of aesthetic response ought to be general enough to cover any aesthetic experience is false. It may be that the nature of response to dance music and the nature of response to a tragic play are irreducibly different, the one triggering off a response by one route, the other setting up a very different response by quite a different route.

The debates around 'form' and 'content' are related and overlap with debates about sensuous and intellectual qualities. For many philosophers, including Kant, aesthetic response is primarily response to form, pattern or structure. It does indeed seem to be the case that it is the pattern of the fields and the contrasts of their colours which makes the Downs attractive to me. And a painting has a similar effect when it displays what Clive Bell in a manifesto of formalism, *Art* (1913), called 'significant form'. But whilst it is true that when I look at the Downs I do not see them as being *about* anything, most works of art (except abstract painting and much music) are about something and this something does appear to be the focus of our imaginative attention: *King Lear* is about Lear, *Tess of the D'Urbervilles* is about Tess, and so on. Again, it could be that 'form' and 'content' are simply differentially important in different works, though it is characteristic of twentieth-century art and art criticism to believe that too much content is a bad thing, not least because it gets in the way of 'pure' aesthetic experience. That said, it is hard to read, say, *Tess* without reflecting on the injustice of the sexual and class relations established in Victorian England, and Thomas Hardy would have been disappointed if his readers were not prompted to such reflection. It is only on a particular view of art that Art and Life should have separate existences.

Some recent criticisms of the medium of photography, due to Roger Scruton, relate in an interesting way to the question of content and will also serve to introduce an aspect of the concern of contemporary aesthetics with differences between the various media of artistic expression and representation. Suppose, then, that one asked, Is there any significant difference between representational paintings and photographs? Both will contain resemblances of what they represent (what they are paintings or photographs *of*) and both consequently belong to the class of *iconic signs*, to use the terminology of the American philosopher, C.S. Peirce (1839–1914). However, they differ in that photographs, unlike paintings, are causally linked to what they are photographs of: photographs originate in light being reflected from an object onto a light-sensitive medium. Peirce calls a sign which is causally linked to its object an *index*, and so the photograph is an indexical sign as well as an iconic one; others have spoken of the photograph as a symptom, trace or record of its object. In contrast, a painting is not an indexical sign; the object does not causally bring it into being. Rather, it is a painter who creates a representation of an object through the intentional action of placing marks on canvas (or whatever).

This difference between painting and photography certainly has a relevance to the old, and by no means dead, question: Can a photograph be a work of art? Scruton, for example, argues in *The Aesthetic Understanding* (1983) that our interest in *what* a photograph shows tends to dominate any aesthetic interest in *how* it shows it; the documentary value which photographs possess in virtue of their causal link to reality actually tends to detract from their aesthetic interest. As it were, photographs have too much content. We inevitably look through the photograph to what it is a photograph of, rather than attend to the photograph itself. This is one reason why, for example, photography can so easily be used in pornography to cause sexual arousal in a way that a painting with identical subject matter cannot or cannot so readily. Photographs can become objects of properly aesthetic interest only insofar as they become more like paintings, which happens when the photographer intervenes between the object and its photograph by means of the manner in which he or she photographs the object. This intervention creates a representation out of something which in its essence is merely a record.

All this, and much more, is controversial and in my view makes aesthetics an increasingly interesting area to study. So too does the fact that the questions considered in Aesthetics connect quite directly with the concerns of people working in neighbouring areas, such as Philosophy of Mind and, outside Philosophy, art history, media and communication studies, literary theory and criticism. C.S. Peirce, for example, as one of the founders of modern semiotics ('the science of signs') is studied as much outside as inside Philosophy departments. Peirce was also one of the founders of modern Logic which, as you may guess, leads me into my next section.

2.10 Logic

For some Philosophers, Logic (Formal Logic) is the heart of Philosophy. For others, it is a highly specialized subject in its own right which is, at best, peripherally relevant to their concerns, but about which students must at least know a little in order to read the works of those Philosophers who are in the habit of decorating their argument with symbols of logical notation. In British higher education, the latter attitude probably still prevails and in treating Logic separately towards the end of my exposition, I am responding to that state of affairs. But what is Logic?

Consider the following story. In the 1930s, the Russian psychologist, A.R. Luria, set out to investigate the effects of literacy on ways of thinking among peasants in Soviet Asia. He would pose the peasants such problems as this, in speech rather than in writing:

Rice only grows in hot countries.
England is a cold country.
Does rice grow in England?

According to Luria (in his book *Cognitive Development: its Cultural and Social Foundations*, translated 1976), literate peasants would readily answer 'No' to the question in the problem above, while illiterate peasants would puzzle over it and reply, 'You can't expect us to know the answer to questions like that' or 'We don't know about rice here' or 'You're the expert. You should be telling us'. These latter replies are comic to us because *we* can see that Luria has in fact provided the peasants with all the information necessary to answering his question. The answer can be *deduced* from the information provided, though the illiterate peasants appear unable to make the deduction which to us seems so easy. Luria's evidence and conclusions are matters of controversy, but the story does allow me to indicate what Logic is. For we can say that the fact that the answer to Luria's question can be deduced from the information he has provided is a consequence of the form in which that information is given. We recognize this form intuitively when we realize that we can generate an indefinite number of examples formally identical to Luria's, for instance:

Polar bears are found only in cold countries
Nigeria is a hot country
Are polar bears found in Nigeria?

Logic is concerned with isolating the patterns or forms implicit in sentences insofar as those patterns (often called 'logical form') are relevant to the arguments or inferences which can be validly derived from information the sentences present. Equally, Logic is concerned with giving an account of valid argument or inference in terms of formulating rules which ensure that if the information initially provided (the premisses of an argument) is true, then any conclusions drawn from it will also be true. Logicians express this concept of validity by saying that valid arguments are *truth-preserving*.

Logical form and logical validity can be studied quite apart from any psychological assumptions about people's actual reasoning abilities, and since the work of Frege logicians have generally been keen to insist that Logic has nothing to do with psychology, with how we actually think. C.S. Peirce, for example, conceived Logic as a normative science concerned with the standards of valid reasoning, not with whether or not people do reason correctly. Equally, because Logic is concerned with the form of information and argument, it can and does represent those forms in one or other notation, or symbol system, which abstracts from the particularities of individual examples of information and argument. But it should not be thought that doing this is a straightforward business. There are problems both in establishing what the logical form of a sentence is and about the validity of different forms of inference. Many logicians, in fact, doubt that ordinary-language arguments can be satisfactorily formalized and think that Logic is needed more to replace than to reflect everyday inference. Such issues are discussed in courses on the Philosophy of Logic (sometimes, as at Oxford, misleadingly known as Philosophical Logic). In terms of the relationship between Logic and Philosophy, some Philosophers are inclined to say that it is only when we fully understand a problem that we can proceed to state its abstract, logical structure. Consequently, the symbolisms of Logic are not very much help to Philosophers characteristically concerned with problems the problematic feature of which is that we are not sure how to state them. Friends of formal logic will riposte that there would be fewer failed arguments in Philosophy if Philosophers submitted themselves to the discipline of formalizing their arguments.

To give a foretaste of the content of Logic, I will in the remainder of this section discuss how one might go about representing in what is called *Standard Predicate Calculus* the information Luria provided to his peasants, and indicate what rules define the inferences by which we can derive a true answer to his question. For more rigorous and complete introductions to Logic, I refer the reader to any one of the textbooks of Logic listed in Appendix A, Part 2. These normally introduce Logic through what is known as *Propositional Calculus*, which handles whole propositions without decomposing them into consitituent elements.

Looking at the statement, 'Rice only grows in hot countries', the logician would probably start by noting that it says something about countries, in fact, about all of them. Countries are the subject of the statement, and countries form the domain from which substitution instances for the predicate calculus variable, x, can be drawn. The fact that 'countries' means 'all countries' can be represented by the logician's universal quantifier, ($\forall$), which means 'All'. The statement says of all countries that they will only have one property, ability to grow rice (call this property, F), if they have another property, hotness (call it G). F and G are things we can predicate of x. We can now represent the form of 'Rice only grows in hot countries' as follows:

(1) $(\forall x) (Fx \rightarrow Gx)$

This is to be read as saying that, 'For all x, F is a property of x only if G is a property of x since the arrow ($\rightarrow$) means, roughly, 'only if'. I say 'roughly' because one of the problems of translating from ordinary language to predicate calculus is that the meaning of '$\rightarrow$' is not defined in terms of ordinary-language equivalents but rather in terms of the truth-conditions of the formulae in which it figures. Thus, (1) will be reckoned a false claim about a state of the world only when Fx is true and Gx is false. For all other cases, including the case where Fx is false and Gx true, the claim embodied in (1) will be reckoned true.

The claim that 'England is a cold country' can be converted to 'England is not a hot country' provided we have the semantic knowledge that 'cold' and 'hot' are opposites or contraries, the truth of either excluding the truth of the other. If we let 'a' stand for England, then the claim that 'England is not a hot country' can be rewritten as (2):

(2) $- Ga$

(2) is to be read as saying 'It is not the case that G is a property of a', since the ' $-$ ' is the sign for negation.

(1) and (2) together form the premises of the argument. From (1) we can derive (3) by a rule known as Universal Quantifier Elimination:

(3) $Fa \rightarrow Ga$

(3), in effect, particularizes the general claim about countries to one particular country, England. Universal Quantifier Elimination permits the inference of a singular argument from a universal one. Then, from the conjunction of (2) and (3) we can derive (4) by a rule known as Modus Tollendo Tollens, which derives the negation of the antecedent from that of the consequent:

(4) $-Fa$

But (4) simply represents the claim that England does not have property F, the ability to grow rice – and this is the answer to Luria's question as well as the conclusion of the logical deduction. That the logic deployed here should be called a calculus will not surprise anyone who has studied 'ordinary' calculus as part of mathematics and it is, indeed, worth noting that Frege pioneered what we now know as Standard Predicate Calculus as part of his endeavour to reduce the laws of arithmetic to those of logic, an approach known as logicism.

Predicate calculus allows the formal presentation of arguments involving the quantities *all* and *some* and which predicate properties or concepts like 'hot', of objects or singular terms like 'England'. Other logics allow the formalization and representation of arguments involving concepts of necessity and possibility (modal logic); knowledge and belief (epistemic logic); ought and can (deontic logic), and so on through several other increasingly exotic varieties. In each case, the most common aim is to construct a calculus such that all and only those arguments which come out as valid according to the rules of the calculus are also intuitively or pre-theoretically valid in commonsense reasoning or in some branch of science, such as mathematics or physics. Not all of these logics will be encountered in undergraduate courses in Philosophy, though some of them will become familiar to students of linguistics and artificial intelligence where they have proved to be of relevance – a fact which encourages me to encourage those, like myself, with no taste for symbol manipulation to persist at least far enough to acquaint themselves with what goes on in Logic and not to give up on it too readily as something 'not for me'.

2.11 Modern continental Philosophy

For the British student, 'modern continental Philosophy' generally means study of a selection of authors and themes which have not been integrated into the main divisions of Philosophy as I have presented them, but which are felt to have a place in a Philosophy course. It must be said that there are, first of all, modern German-language (though not French-language) Philosophers whose work *is* fully integrated into the mainstream of Philosophy teaching. This is true of Frege and Wittgenstein, for example, whose work actually defines many of the concerns of current Philosophy of Language and Mind. Second, however, there are other continental Philosophers, some of whose themes are identical or parallel to those of concern to analytical Philosophers, yet whose work for one reason or another remains largely unintegrated into the appropriate courses and is treated independently as modern continental Philosophy. This is true, for example, of most of the work of Husserl, Heidegger and Sartre. Third, and finally, there are continental Philosophers whose work is generally perceived as having little or no bearing on typical Anglo-American concerns and which therefore has to be read from a fresh perspective or else simply ignored. This is the case with much of recent French Philosophy, as practised by such figures as Jacques Derrida, Gilles Deleuze and Jean-François Lyotard. This is not to say that there is no dispute about how to read or whether to ignore Philosophers in the second and third categories: John Searle may regard Derrida as a charlatan; Richard Rorty, author of the influential *Philosophy and the Mirror of Nature* (1980) does not.

The principal philosophical schools or movements which the student will encounter under the heading of modern continental Philosophy are Phenomenology, Existentialism, Structuralism and Post-Structuralism.

Phenomenology now generally refers to that approach to philosophy developed by Edmund Husserl and his followers, including those such as Martin Heidegger whose work really diverges quite radically from Husserl's. Husserl's central concern was with the contents of the mind, and in particular with the description and analysis of those mental phenomena which possess *intentionality*. 'Intentionality' refers to the directedness of the mind on objects which need not actually exist: I can equally well have a fear of snakes, which do exist; a fear of ghosts, which may not; and a fear of the bogeyman, who does not exist. In each case, the mind is similarly directed towards the object of fear and Husserl thought that such intentional states or acts and their objects could be fully analysed without raising or settling the question of whether the objects really exist; this question, Husserl claimed, could be bracketed or suspended and our attention focused on describing the phenomena as they appear to us – hence the name 'Phenomenology'. Phenomenological description is claimed to be non-empirical or *a priori* and Husserl claims that through it we can intuit the essences, the defining characteristics, of the phenomena we are investigating. Thus, for example, in a study of *The Phenomenology of Internal Time Consciousness* (1928; written *c.* 1905), Husserl sought to articulate the way in which our experience of time is not the experience of a series of disconnected instants but essentially an experience of something which comes out of a past and goes into a future. In another area, one of Husserl's students, Roman Ingarden (1893–1970) set out in his *Literary Work of Art* (1931) to offer a phenomenological account of the experience of reading literature and the nature of the work which is read – analysing, for example, the way that in imagination we concretize the schematic information which the text of a novel provides. It is this concretization which makes it the case that when we see the film of the book we are often led to say such things as 'That's not how I imagined her', without thereby necessarily implying that either we or the film maker got her wrong.

As these two examples illustrate, Phenomenology has to do with phenomena as subjectively experienced by individuals. It thus belongs to the Cartesian and Kantian traditions, which adopt 'first-person' perspectives on questions of mind and knowledge. As much as Descartes or Kant, Husserl is committed to the existence of a transcendental subject or ego who has the experiences which Phenomenology seeks to describe. Much of more recent modern continental Philosophy is a reaction against the subjectivism of Phenomenology and, ultimately, against the idea of a transcendental subject. Heidegger, for example, in his major work, *Being and Time* (1927) seeks to shift the emphasis away from mind and knowledge towards Ontology, that is, the theory of what exists or, in Heidegger's terms, the doctrine of Being. And the idea of a subject prior to, independent of, yet unifying our experience is attacked in Structuralism and Post-Structuralism. But these latter – mainly French – approaches in Philosophy are also reactions against (mainly French) Existentialism, and I must first of all say a little about that.

Existentialism may be characterized as a vision of the human predicament which emphasizes the ever-renewed need for human beings to make choices in an unpredictable world, a world in which God either does not exist or, at least, is not manifest. In addition, it is perhaps the key existentialist idea that it is through their choices that human beings make themselves the persons that they are: against any kind of essentialism of human nature, existentialists believe, in a slogan, that *existence precedes essence*. This doctrine has a critical edge to it, for existentialists characteristically argue that people in fact seek to avoid the anguishing recognition of their freedom and the ever-renewed obligation to choose. Description and exposure of such evasion is a prominent feature of the existentialist writings of Kierkegaard, Heidegger and, most famously, Sartre. When the obscurer doctrines of his *Being and Nothingness* (1943) are forgotten, everyone remembers Sartre's depictions of bad faith (*mauvaise foi*): the waiter who pretends to be a waiter in an (unsuccessful) attempt to avoid realizing that he *makes* himself one; the woman who acts as if her companion's hand was not on her knee, thereby seeking to evade making a choice between permitting or refusing a seduction. In Sartre, the point of these vivid portraits is to recall the reader to a sense of his or her own freedom and responsibility. In 1943, when *Being and Nothingness* was published, that implied, in particular, facing up to decisions between collaborating with the German occupation of France and supporting the Resistance to it. Shortly after, Simone de Beauvoir (1908–86) enlisted Existentialism in the cause of feminism. In her *The Second Sex* (1949) the slogan that existence precedes essence becomes the critical idea that one is not born a woman; one becomes one. Again, in what has become known as existential psychoanalysis, the key distinction is made between *process* and *practice*, between things which happen to us and things which we do, and the way in which we disguise practice as process (in hysteria, for example). And this distinction, too, has an obvious critical edge to it. As all these examples illustrate, Existentialism is a philosophy of commitment and engagement and this has been its attraction to those dissatisfied with more dispassionate styles of Philosophy, whether continental or Anglo-American. But Structuralism and Post-Structuralism are strong reactions against its characteristically humanist assertion of the centrality of the world-making individual, and to these more recent philosophies I now turn.

In fact, I shall illustrate these philosophies through consideration of one of their shared themes, ignoring what divides them (indeed, the term 'Post-Structuralism' signals that it has no independently characterizable status). The theme is that of the *constitution and identity of the subject* – what in Anglo-American Philosophy would figure in the Philosophy of Mind as the problem of the self. The general position on this theme espoused by structuralist and post-structuralist philosophies is nicely caught by two of my colleagues, Peter Stallybrass and Allon White, who in their book on *The Politics and Poetics of Transgression* (1986) write that 'identity is discursively produced from the moment of entry into language'. What does this mean, and how is this view – which can be found disseminated through much recent work in literary and feminist theory – arrived at?

In Phenomenology, as I have indicated above, the self or ego is conceived as something prior to and independent of experience – as a transcendental subject. This is a view which Hume rejected when he expressed himself unable to catch himself without a perception, and which led him to dissolve or reduce the self into its experiences and their connections. But both Husserl's and Hume's approach have in common that they ignore or deny any part that *other* people might have in making me the self or subject that I am. It is the idea that self and others are interdependent, not independent, which is taken up systematically by Hegel, among earlier philosophers, and which has been re-developed in structuralist and post-structuralist thinking. Thus Hegel had written, in *The Phenomenology of Spirit* (1807) that 'self-consciousness exists in itself and for itself, insofar as and by virtue of the fact that it exists for another self-consciousness; that is, it *is* only by being acknowledged or recognized.' That such recognition takes place centrally in the medium of language is a characteristically modern view, though prefigured in Rousseau's claim that 'Who says man says language, and who says language says society' (in the *Essay on the Origin of Languages*, 1755). Among recent thinkers who have developed and radicalized these insights, one can single out for mention the French psychoanalyst-philosopher, Jacques Lacan (1900–80), who expounds the view that it is only through becoming users of a language that pre-exists us and is preconstructed or pre-structured for us that we become self-conscious subjects; and it is from Lacan among others that Stallybrass and White derive their view that our identity is produced discursively, that is, in the practice of using language.

Like the Existentialism to which it opposes itself, this structuralist and post-structuralist theory of the subject has a critical cutting edge. For it implies, when fleshed out, that our sense of self-identity, that I am what I am and that this is what makes me myself, can be shown to be an illusion, something imaginary. For the self which I identify myself with is something produced in me, through language, by others, by society – for all that I experience myself as a locus of responsibility and freedom. It is this critique or deconstruction of the self as subject which defines a great deal of contemporary French philosophy as anti-humanist, in conscious opposition to the existentialist humanism of Sartre, and which also marks it as sceptical and relativist, aligned with the critical, suspicious theories of Marx, Nietzsche and Freud (1856–1938) in opposition to the confident, absolutist positions of Descartes, Kant and Husserl. This critical edge to the 'theory of the subject' is the source of its appeal to many writers, and the impact of the theory reverberates through much contemporary political, sociological, psychoanalytic and literary theory.

My own view, for what it is worth, is that this widely deployed theory of the subject in fact belongs to a criticizable reductivist approach to philosophy. Just as debunking-minded Philosophers are inclined to say things like, 'This table does not exist because tables are only matter in motion' – thereby reducing one thing (a table) to another (matter in motion) – so debunking post-structuralists deny the reality of the subject: 'You are only an effect of language (and, hence, society)'. The trouble is that this view uses a third-person, objective approach to undermine a first-person, subjective one: a theory of what it *is* to be a human subject (which may be true) is used to undermine our sense of what it *is like* to be a human subject or person. But there is no reason why we should accept to have the subjective view undercut in this reductivist way, any more than we should cease believing in the existence of tables once we know about matter in motion. That the question, What is it to be a subject or person?, is quite different from the question, What is it like to be a subject or person?, is nicely brought out in the context of Anglo-American Philosophy by Thomas Nagel in his essay, 'What is it like to be a bat?' (1974).

The last remark does, of course, imply that in my view even the latest movements in modern continental Philosophy can be brought into relation with Anglo-American analytical Philosophy, if we make the effort. But as I have implied in my initial indication of allegiance (see Chapter 1, p. 9), I do not think that, brought into such a relation, that modern continental Philosophy will always stand up to critical scrutiny: they do not necessarily order these things better in France.

2.12 Other branches of Philosophy

Inevitably, in this thumbnail sketch of the branches of Philosophy, as the undergraduate student is likely to encounter them, much has been left out. In addition, material which has been referred to here under one heading will often turn up in courses under another heading. This is notably the case when courses are offered which are devoted to named individuals, or philosophical schools. So at my own University, Sussex, much of the material I mention under 'Metaphysics' and 'Epistemology' will turn up in a two-term course entitled 'Descartes to Kant'. At Sussex, other philosophers merit courses named after them, currently Plato, Aristotle, Hegel, Marx and Wittgenstein.

In addition, the Sussex undergraduate has available for study as options courses with titles such as 'Philosophy of History' and 'Philosophy of Religion'. Indeed, 'Philosophy of . . .' courses are indefinitely extendible. They commonly include Philosophy of Law and Philosophy of Education. In the United States, it would not be uncommon to find option courses in the Philosophy of Sport or the Philosophy of Sex. All such 'Philosophy of . . .' courses tend to have as their content a very general study of the nature of an area of human activity and of controversial questions which do not obviously lend themselves to resolution of the basis of observation and experiment. Here, for example, are one or two questions which might arise in the study of each of the possible

'Philosophy of . . .' courses I have mentioned:
- Is there progress in history?
  Is the study of history a science?
- Does God exist?
  Can the existence of suffering in the world be reconciled with the idea that God is both all good and all powerful?
- Are there any natural rights?
  Should judges be able to make law?
- What is education?
  Can indoctrination be avoided?
- Is competitive sport a desirable activity?
- Are all sexual acts between consenting partners morally equal?

And so on. It should be clear from this short list of questions that questions in 'Philosophy of . . .' courses will often relate directly to questions in the core areas of Philosophy, such as Metaphysics or Moral Philosophy, and the 'Philosophy of . . .' course will often take the form of an application of ideas established elsewhere. For this reason, 'Philosophy of . . .' courses generally appear as options, and not always highly regarded options: for example, Philosophers can be, and have been, very rude about the Philosophy of Education; so, Honderich and Burnyeat exclude the subject from their anthology, *Philosophy As It Is*, on the grounds that it 'has not since John Dewey (1859–1952) been in touch with the mainstream of philosophy'. Very few British Philosophers have wanted to tangle with areas like the Philosophy of Sport and Philosophy of Sex (exceptions are David Best in his *Philosophy and Human Movement* (1978) and Roger Scruton in his *Sexual Desire* (1986)). Despite the importance of sport and sex in people's lives, British Philosophers have been inclined to see such areas as suitable for study only in American supermarket universities. In other words, as in any other subject, Philosophers not only place each other in a hierarchy of achievement but also discriminate within their subject between high and low prestige areas, the high prestige areas being those also conceived as representing the core of the subject as currently thought and taught.

3
The uses of Philosophy

Most students give up Philosophy when given their BAs. In some ways, this outcome is disturbing: if you chose to study a subject out of interest, why should you not continue to be interested after graduation? In other ways, it is not: our interests change and it doesn't matter that the Philosophy which intrigued us at 18 doesn't intrigue us at 28. All that matters is that *something* still intrigues us. Again, if as I have said, Philosophy is hard, then the teacher, social worker, manager or computer programmer is going to look elsewhere for pleasure at the end of a hard day's work. These soothing considerations do not entirely satisfy me, and I would not want to discount either the claim that some Philosophy teaching puts people off the subject or the claim that it's just not very sensible for even small numbers of young people to be encouraged to spend three years studying a fairly esoteric subject at an age when other things are probably more important to them. Much better to spread out Philosophy more thinly over a liberal adult education programme available to much larger numbers of people over the course of a lifetime. On such issues you will have your own ideas. It remains for me only to say something about the vocational relevance of Philosophy.

First, of course, some students of Philosophy will become teachers of Philosophy. But probably very few. In schools, it is unlikely that the teaching of Philosophy will expand greatly, even though there has been quite a lot of interest in the new Philosophy 'A' levels with 385 candidates sitting the AEB's exam in 1986. Though some Philosophers are actually opposed to the teaching of Philosophy in schools, fearing dilution or perversion of the subject, there is probably enough sympathy for the subject and for the plight of unemployed Philosophers to allow a modest expansion in the teaching of Philosophy at 'A' level and, perhaps, earlier.

In universities and polytechnics, there is unlikely to be much expansion in Philosophy teaching in the next few years. Indeed, in the universities, Philosophy has been contracted in recent cut-backs, with the number of posts in the subject reduced from 400 to 320 in the first half of the 1980s. At the time of writing (late 1986), the closure of Philosophy departments in several Universities is being actively considered. The department at Surrey has already been closed. Furthermore, the age structure of the teaching force in higher education is such that very few replacements due to retirement will be required for 10 to 20 years. In this context, unemployed Philosophers have formed themselves into a self-help group, PLATO (Philosophers' Lecturing and Teaching Opportunities) which seeks to provide alternative outlets for the talents of Philosophers who find that there simply are no full-time permanent appointments in their subject.

For the great majority of Philosophy graduates who are not seeking jobs as Philosophers. employment prospects are quite good. Indeed, if the Royal Institute of Philosophy (RIP) is to be believed, Philosophy is not a bad choice of degree subject for anyone concerned with employability and, indeed, vocational relevance. For, according to a 1986 RIP survey (*Philosophy Graduates and Jobs* by Peter Ratcliffe and Martin Warner) of 1,357 Philosophy students graduating in 1980–82, over half of the 539 respondents claimed never to have been unemployed since graduation and three-quarters claim now to be in long-term employment. Eight per cent say they are jobless. Of the 468 respondents answering the relevant question, 15.1 per cent are teaching – though only a handful teach Philosophy. 'Administrative' work occupies 12.4 per cent of the graduates, 6.6 per cent are in social work, 10.4 per cent in accountancy and finance, and 11.7 per cent in computer work of some kind – more about this last group in a moment. Eighty seven per cent of those in employment say that they are satisfied with their current job.

Interestingly, for my purposes, over half the respondents said that Philosophy had proved helpful in career terms, with just 6.6 per cent saying that Philosophy had proved irrelevant or a positive hindrance. Nearly a quarter (121) of respondents felt that employers had a positive view of Philosophy, compared with 45 who felt employers regarded the subject with doubt or scorn. Employers taking a positive view probably think, as is often claimed on its behalf, that Philosophy develops paticular skills in identifying and critically analysing the structures of arguments of various kinds. Those who thought Philosophy was of positive interest to employers in fact singled out Logic and Philosophy of Mind as the branches in which their employers were interested, with Logic being of notable interest to the employers of graduates in the field of computer-related activities.

Indeed, it is true that in recent years, graduates in Philosophy have found themselves quite highly employable in the area of computer-related work, where there have been shortages of suitable workers. The relevance of Philosophy to this area arises from the fact that many of the problems faced in programming computers to undertake activities which would require intelligence if performed by humans are similar or identical to problems considered in the philosophy of mind and language, in the theory of knowledge, and in logic. For Philosophy graduates with a taste for those areas of Philosophy and an interest in the world of computers, there are currently good opportunities of employment. And in some Universities, including my own, it is possible to combine the study of Philosophy with work in Artificial Intelligence and related areas. When they think of the origins of their subject, Philosophers think of Socrates standing arguing in the public spaces of ancient Athens. When they think of their present, Philosophers usually picture themselves conversing from a comfortable armchair. It may be that the appropriate image for the Philosopher of the future is that of someone who faces away from us and towards the VDU screen which links them to the intellectual world of the computer. Many Philosophers would, however, be horrified by this idea.

Appendix A. Bibliography and further reading

This Appendix is in two parts. Part 1 lists in alphabetical order all works mentioned in the text and gives publication details of available editions. Where several editions are available, I have usually singled out what seems to me to be the most accessible, reliable one. Dates of original publication are given in the main text, and are not repeated here. Part 2 is a list of suggestions for Further Reading. Most of the works listed are readily available in paperback. However, the date which follows the publisher's name is the date of original publication, not the date of any paperback edition, though where the hardback and paperback have different publishers, it is the publisher of the paperback which I list.

Part 1 Bibliography

Ayer, A.J. *Language, Truth and Logic*. Penguin.

Beauvoir, S. de *The Second Sex*. Penguin.

Bell, C. *Art*. Perigee Books (G.P. Putnam's Sons, New York).

Berkeley, G. *Three Dialogues Between Hylas and Philonus* in his *Philosophical Works* ed. M.R. Ayres. Dent/Everyman.

Best, D. *Philosophy and Human Movement*. Allen & Unwin.

Buchanan, A. 'Revolutionary Motivation and Rationality' in *Philosophy and Public Affairs*, vol. 9, no. 1, 1979.

Burge, T. 'Individualism and The Mental' in P. French et al., eds., *Midwest Studies in Philosophy, volume IV*, pp 73–121. University of Minnesota Press.

Castaneda, C. *The Teachings of Don Juan: a Yaqui way of Knowledge*. Penguin.

Dennett, D. *Elbow Room*. Oxford University Press.

Descartes, R. *Discourse on Method* in his *Philosophical Writings* ed. E. Anscombe and P. Geach. Nelson.

Dworkin, R. *Law's Empire*. Fontana Press.

Hegel, G. *The Phenomenology of Spirit*. Trans. A.V. Miller. Oxford University Press.

Heidegger, M. *Being and Time* trans. J. Macquarrie and E. Robinson. SCM Press/Basil Blackwell.

Hobbes, T. *Leviathan* ed. C.B. Macpherson. Penguin.

Honderich, T. and Burnyeat, M. eds., *Philosophy As It Is*. Penguin.

Hume, D. *A Treatise of Human Nature* ed. P.H. Nidditch. Oxford University Press.

Husserl, E. *The Phenomenology of Internal Time Consciousness*, trans. J.S. Churchill. Martinus Nijhoff, The Hague.

Ingarden, R. *The Literary Work of Art* trans. G. Grabowicz. Northwestern University Press.

Journal of Applied Philosophy. Published by the Society for Applied Philosophy.

Kant, I. *Critique of Pure Reason*, trans. and ed. N. Kemp Smith. Macmillan.

Kant, I. *The Critique of Judgement*, trans. J.C. Meredith. Oxford University Press.

Kuhn, T. *The Structure of Scientific Revolutions*. University of Chicago Press.

Luria, A.R. *Cognitive Development: its cultural and social foundations*. Harvard University Press.

MacIntyre, A. *After Virtue*. Duckworth.

Marx, K. and Engels, F. *The Communist Manifesto* in K. Marx and F. Engels, *Selected Works* and numerous other collections. Lawrence & Wishart.

Mill, J.S. *On Liberty* in J.S. Mill, *Three Essays* ed. R. Wollheim. Oxford University Press. Or separately, ed. G. Himmelfarb. Penguin.

Mill, J.S. *The Subjection of Women*. In J.S. Mill, *Three Essays* ed. R. Wollheim. Oxford University Press. Alternatively in *Enfranchisement of Women*, ed. K. Soper. Virago.

Nagel, T. 'What is It Like To Be a Bat?', in his *Mortal Questions*. Cambridge University Press.

O'Hear, A. *What Philosophy is*. Penguin.

Olson, M. *The Logic of Collective Action*. Harvard University Press.

Philosophy and Public Affairs. Published by Princeton University Press.

Plato *The Complete Dialogues*, eds. E. Hamilton and H. Cairns. Princeton University Press. There are numerous editions of the individual dialogues.

Popper, K. *The Logic of Scientific Discovery*. Routledge & Kegan Paul.

Quine, W. *Word and Object*. Massachusetts Institute of Technology Press.

Rawls, J. *A Theory of Justice*. Oxford University Press.

Ratcliffe, P. and Warner, M. *Philosophy Graduates and Jobs*. The

Royal Institute of Philosophy and the University of Warwick.

Rorty, R. *Philosophy and the Mirror of Nature*. Basil Blackwell.

Rousseau, J.-J. *The Social Contract* in *The Social Contract and Discourses*, eds. G. Cole, J. Brumfitt and J. Hall. Dent/Everyman.

Rousseau, J.-J. *Essay on the Origin of Languages*. In J. Moran and A. Gode eds., *On The Origin of Language*. University of Chicago Press.

Russell, B. *The Problems of Philosophy*. Oxford University Press.

Sartre, J.-P. *Being and Nothingness*, trans. H. Barnes. Methuen.

Scruton, R. *Sexual Desire*. Weidenfeld & Nicolson.

Scruton, R. *The Aesthetic Understanding*. Methuen.

Searle, J. *Minds, Brains and Science*. British Broadcasting Corporation.

Searle, J. *Intentionality*. Cambridge University Press.

Skinner, B.F. *Beyond Freedom and Dignity*. Jonathan Cape.

Stallybrass, P. and White, A. *The Politics and Poetics of Transgression*. Methuen.

Wittgenstein, L. *Philosophical Investigations*. Basil Blackwell.

Part 2   Further reading

Mine is not the only introductory guide to Philosophy. See also Martin Hollis, *Invitation to Philosophy* (Blackwell 1985).

Excellent, cheap and short paperback introductions to the great philosophers of the past are to be had in the Oxford University Press's *Past Masters* series and the Fontana Press's *Modern Masters* series. The former has volumes devoted to most of the major figures in philosophy from Plato to Marx. The latter covers Russell, Popper, Wittgenstein and such modern continental philosophers as Heidegger and Sartre. Penguin Books publish a good study of *Wittgenstein* by Anthony Kenny (1973). A good, historically oriented introduction to philosophy is Roger Scruton's *A Short History of Modern Philosophy from Descartes to Wittgenstein* (Ark 1984).

For an introduction to Philosophy oriented to problems and contemporary work rather than the history of philosophy I recommend Anthony O'Hear's, *What Philosophy Is* (Penguin 1985) – hard going in parts. For someone who wants to read some Philosophy as it is now practised rather than written up for outsiders, I recommend Ted Honderich and Myles Burnyeat, eds., *Philosophy As It Is* (Penguin 1979). In the same style, Oxford University Press publish a large and valuable series, *Oxford Readings in Philosophy*, each volume of which is a collection of article-length studies by different authors. The standard, though by now rather dated, seven-volume encyclopaedic reference work is Paul Edwards, editor, *The Encyclopaedia of Philosophy* (Free Press 1967).

General introductions or individually outstanding works related to the branches of Philosophy which I have distinguished are listed below. As noted above, I give the date of original publication, ignoring second editions etc., but give the publisher of the currently available edition (in paperback where there is a paperback).

Metaphysics

A.J. Ayer – *Language Truth and Logic* (1936). Penguin.
B. Russell – *The Problems of Philosophy* (1912). Oxford University Press.
P.F. Strawson – *Skepticism and Naturalism: Some Varieties* (1985). Methuen.

Epistemology

A.J. Ayer – *The Problem of Knowledge* (1956). Penguin.
R. Chisholm – *Theory of Knowledge* (1966). Prentice-Hall.

Philosophy of Science

T. Kuhn – *The Structure of Scientific Revolutions* (1962). University of Chicago Press.
K. Popper – *Conjectures and Refutations* (1969). Routledge & Kegan Paul.
K. Popper – *Unended Quest* (1974). Fontana.

Philosophy of Language

S. Blackburn – *Spreading the Word* (1984). Oxford University Press.
B. Harrison – *An Introduction to the Philosophy of Language* (1979). Macmillan.
M. Platts – *Ways of Meaning* (1979). Routledge & Kegan Paul.

Philosophy of Mind

P. Churchland – *Matter and Consciousness* (1985). Massachusetts Institute of Technology Press.
C. McGinn – *The Character of Mind* (1982). Oxford University Press.
J. Searle – *Minds, Brains and Science* (1984). BBC Publications.

Moral Philosophy

T. Honderich – *Punishment: The Supposed Justifications* (1969). Penguin.

A. MacIntyre – *A Short History of Ethics* (1967). Routledge & Kegan Paul.
J. Mackie – *Ethics* (1977). Penguin.

Political Philosophy

R. Nozick – *Anarchy, State and Utopia* (1974). Blackwell.
J. Rawls – *A Theory of Justice* (1970). Oxford University Press.
(These are both major works. The key chapters are excerpted in Honderich and Burnyeat's *Philosophy As It Is*. See also A. Brown – *Modern Political Philosophy* (1986). Penguin.

Aesthetics

M. Beardsley – *Aesthetics: Problems in the Philosophy of Criticism* (1958). Hackett Publishing, USA.
R. Scruton – *The Aesthetic Understanding* (1983). Methuen.
R. Wollheim – *Art and Its Objects* (1969). Cambridge University Press.

Logic

S. Haack – *Philosophy of Logics* (1978). Cambridge University Press.
W. Hodges – *Logic* (1977). Penguin.
E.J. Lemmon – *Beginning Logic* (1965). Nelson.
W. Newton-Smith – *Logic* (1985). Routledge & Kegan Paul.

Modern Continental Philosophy

V. Descombes – *Modern French Philosophy* (1980). Cambridge University Press.
J.-J. Lecercle – *Philosophy Through the Looking Glass* (1985). Hutchinson.
J.-P. Sartre – *Existentialism and Humanism* (1946). Methuen.

Finally, for expressions of discontent with current Anglo-American institutionalized Philosophy, see
R. Edgley and P. Osborne, eds., – *The Radical Philosophy Reader* (1985). Verso.

Appendix B. Choosing an undergraduate course in Philosophy

Volume 1 of *Which Degree*? published by New Opportunity Press lists all single-subject Philosophy degree courses available in the UK, together with all courses in which Philosophy figures as a joint subject. In 1985–86 Philosophy was available in single-subject degree courses at 38 university institutions and one polytechnic (North London). Joint courses were available in 40 university institutions and 5 non-university institutions. Clearly, there is no shortage of courses to choose among, and the joint courses allow for combination of Philosophy with virtually any subject you care to name, plus others you didn't know existed (I didn't until I looked through the prospectuses).

So how should one decide where to apply to study Philosophy? If a student's 'A' level profile and geographical mobility allow him or her some choice, and once a decision has been made about the kind of university of polytechnic he or she wishes to study at (using *The Sunday Times Good University Guide* and similar publications), then the following are probably relevant criteria to use in selecting a Philosophy department:

How big is the Department of Philosophy?

Most Philosophy departments are small, with 5 to 7 full-time, permanent members of Faculty. Though there are advantages to small departments – you get to know everyone, everyone knows you, and so on – there are disadvantages. Not all lecturers are lively and up-to-date and that implies that a small department may really be even smaller in terms of stimulating teaching. Equally, it is harder for a small department to cater for all interests, and you may find there is no one to respond to your particular passion. Personally, I would avoid a very small department, especially one top-heavy with Professors and Readers nearing retirement. Not least, in the current climate it may well be scheduled for closure – whether such a possibility exists is, indeed, one you might (tactfully) pose at interview. That said, I should also say that university Philosophers are, in general, strongly in favour of having a Philosophy presence in every university and are currently lobbying in support of that position. Still, for myself, I would prefer a larger Department with eight or more members of faculty, if I had the choice.

Oxford and Cambridge each boast dozens of Philosophers, but remember that normal teaching is College-based and you could be as badly off as in a dull, small department, except that there will also be University-wide lecture courses available, often given by outstanding Philosophers. In other universities, variety of the kind Oxford and Cambridge can offer is often partially provided for by having visiting speakers to address a Philosophy Society. At interview, it would be worth asking whether a Philosophy Society exists.

How prestigious is the Department?

University teachers are expected to research and publish. Good research does not necessarily imply good teaching, but a good research record does mark out a Department as 'where it's at'. It is worth knowing that in May 1986 the University Grants Committee rated all university Philosophy departments on the basis of their research record, using four categories: 'Outstanding', 'Above average', 'Average' and 'Below average'. The ratings are controversial, and may date, but I give below the location of departments rated 'Outstanding' or 'Above average':

> *Outstanding*
> Bristol
> Cambridge
> Essex
> King's College, London
> University College, London
> Oxford
>
> *Above Average*
> Birkbeck College, London
> Glasgow
> Lancaster
> St Andrew's
> Stirling
> Swansea

No comparable assessments are available on the few polytechnic institutions which offer Philosophy courses, though Philosophy at the Polytechnic of North London and Middlesex Polytechnic is well-established and, I think, well-respected.

Does the Department offer anything unusual that might appeal to me?

Joint courses allow vast numbers of Philosophy-with-something-else combinations. Some institutions claim to offer a Philosophy which is itself in some way different. So, for example, Belfast emphasizes the history of Philosophy and contemporary European Philosophy; Cardiff allows the study of Philosophy as History of Ideas; Warwick has an exchange scheme with an American University; Sussex offers Philosophy in the context of artificial intelligence (Cognitive Studies); Scottish Universities offer four-year programmes leading to the degree of MA. And so on. Only a detailed study of the Prospectuses of individual institutions will tell you what you need to know about the particular kind of Philosophy on offer.

Index